CW01072179

Portuguese

An Essential Guide to Portuguese Language Learning

© Copyright 2018

All rights Reserved. No part of this book may be reproduced in any form without permission in writing from the author. Reviewers may quote brief passages in reviews.

Disclaimer: No part of this publication may be reproduced or transmitted in any form or by any means, mechanical or electronic, including photocopying or recording, or by any information storage and retrieval system, or transmitted by email without permission in writing from the publisher.

While all attempts have been made to verify the information provided in this publication, neither the author nor the publisher assumes any responsibility for errors, omissions or contrary interpretations of the subject matter herein.

This book is for entertainment purposes only. The views expressed are those of the author alone, and should not be taken as expert instruction or commands. The reader is responsible for his or her own actions.

Adherence to all applicable laws and regulations, including international, federal, state and local laws governing professional licensing, business practices, advertising and all other aspects of doing business in the US, Canada, UK or any other jurisdiction is the sole responsibility of the purchaser or reader.

Neither the author nor the publisher assumes any responsibility or liability whatsoever on the behalf of the purchaser or reader of these materials. Any perceived slight of any individual or organization is purely unintentional.

Contents

INTRODUCTION **8**

CHAPTER 1 – GETTING TO KNOW THE PORTUGUESE LANGUAGE . 9

1.1 THE PORTUGUESE ALPHABET 9
    1.1.1 Vowels...*10*
    1.1.2 Consonants *11*
    1.1.3 Combinations...*13*
1.2 ACCENTUATION 15
    1.2.1 Acute accent..*15*
    1.2.2 Grave accent..*16*
    1.2.3 Circumflex accent *16*
    1.2.4 Tilde...*17*
    1.2.5 Cedilla *18*
    1.2.6 Hyphen...*18*
1.3 NOUNS AND ARTICLES 19
1.4 SINGULAR AND PLURAL...22
1.5 MASCULINE AND FEMININE 23
1.6 THE SENTENCE 24
    1.6.1 Structuring a sentence *24*
    1.6.2 Forms of sentences *25*
    1.6.3 Types of sentences *26*

CHAPTER 2 – ADVERBS **29**

2.1 ADVERBS OF TIME 29
2.2 ADVERBS OF PLACE...30
2.3 ADVERBS OF QUANTITY 31
2.4 ADVERBS OF MODE..32
2.5 ADVERBS OF AFFIRMATION 33
2.6 ADVERBS OF NEGATION 33
2.7 ADVERBS OF DOUBT 33
2.8 ADVERBS OF DEMONSTRATION OR DESIGNATION 34

CHAPTER 3 – PRONOUNS **35**

   3.1 PERSONAL PRONOUNS 35
     3.1.1 Straight personal pronouns *35*
     3.1.2 Unstressed oblique personal pronouns *37*
     3.1.3 Stressed oblique personal pronouns.....................*37*
   3.2 POSSESSIVE PRONOUNS 38
   3.3 DEMONSTRATIVE PRONOUNS 40
   3.4 RELATIVE PRONOUNS 43
   3.5 INTERROGATIVE PRONOUNS 43
   3.6 INDEFINITE PRONOUNS 44

CHAPTER 4 – ADJECTIVES.. **45**

   4.1 VARIATION IN GENDER AND NUMBER.............................45
   4.2 DEGREES OF THE ADJECTIVES 46

CHAPTER 5 – PREPOSITIONS.. **50**

   5.1 CONTRACTIONS WITH ARTICLES...................................51

CHAPTER 6 – VERBS **54**

   6.1 CONJUGATIONS 54
   6.3 CONJUGATION OF REGULAR VERBS 61
   6.4 CONJUGATION OF AUXILIARY VERBS 77

CHAPTER 7 – CONJUNCTIONS **94**

   7.1 COORDINATIVE CONJUNCTIONS 94
   7.2 SUBORDINATIVE CONJUNCTIONS 96

CHAPTER 8 – USEFUL EXPRESSIONS AND VOCABULARY **100**

   8.1 MEETING AND GREETING PEOPLE 100
   8.2 INTERJECTIONS 102
   8.3 CARDINAL NUMBERS...103
   8.4 ORDINAL NUMBERS...105
   8.5 TELLING THE TIME 107
   8.6 DATES 108
   8.7 FAMILY 110
   8.8 COLORS 112
   8.10 COUNTRIES AND NATIONALITIES 114
   8.11 PROFESSIONS / JOBS 115
   8.12 GETTING AROUND 116
     8.12.1 At the airport *117*
     8.12.2 In the city *118*
     8.12.3 At the hotel..*120*
     8.12.4 At the bank...*121*

8.12.5 Shopping *122*

8.12.6 At the restaurant *125*

8.12.7 At the hospital *129*

CONCLUSION **132**

PREVIEW OF PORTUGUESE SHORT STORIES **134**

9 SIMPLE AND CAPTIVATING STORIES FOR EFFECTIVE PORTUGUESE LEARNING FOR BEGINNERS *134*

Introduction

More than 200 million native speakers speak the Portuguese language. It is the sixth most spoken language in the world, the third most spoken European language, and it's present in all five continents.

Also, an interesting fact about Portuguese: did you know that Portugal and Brazil have different ways of speaking the language? That's true, but don't worry because this book has got you covered. Throughout the chapters, you'll find several notes and explanations that will guide you, and that will expose the main differences between the two variants.

Learning Portuguese requires work and dedication, just like in any other language, but if you have the passion, everything is easier.

Maybe you're starting from scratch, or maybe you already have a basic knowledge of Portuguese. In either case, this book will fit you perfectly because not only does it presents basic information aimed at beginners, but it also offers some more advanced grammar content.

If learning Portuguese is something you've been delaying for a while or if you simply never had the opportunity to learn it, wait no more. This book is here to help you.

Good luck!

Chapter 1 – Getting to know the Portuguese language

1.1 The Portuguese Alphabet

Until 2009 the Portuguese alphabet had 23 letters. However, when the new Orthographic Agreement came into effect, the alphabet gained three additional letters: K, W, and Y, coming to a total of 26 letters, being 5 vowels and 21 consonants. See the Portuguese alphabet below with the respective pronunciation of each letter in brackets.

A [Ah]

B [Ba(y)]

C [Sa(y)]

D [Da(y)]

E [(Y)eah]

F [Ef]

G [Gé]

H [Uh-gah]

I [Eeh]

J [Jaw-tuh]

K [Kaw-puh] / <u>BR</u>: [Kah]

L [El]

M [Em]

N [En]

O [Aw]

P [Pa(y)]

Q [Ka(y)]

R [Err]

S [Ess]

T [Ta(y)]

U [Oo]

V [Va(y)]

W [Duh-blee-ooh]

X [Cheesh]

Y [Eepslon]

Z [Za(y)]

Note: There's also a special letter, Ç [Sa(y)-duh-cedilla], which we'll talk about in sub-section *1.1.3 Combinations*.

1.1.1 Vowels

There are five vowels: A, E, I, O, and U. Let's talk about each one individually.

The **letter A** may have either an open 'ah' sound (e.g. "fraco", which means "weak"), or a closed 'â' sound (e.g. "antes", which means "before").

The **letter E** may as well be read with an open '(y)eah' sound (e.g. "café", which means "coffee"), or with a closed 'ê' sound (e.g. "caneta", which means "pen").

The **letter I** presents no variation in its pronunciation. It is always read with an 'ee' sound (e.g. "filho", which means "son").

The **letter O** may be read with an open 'aw' sound (e.g. "corte", which means "cut"), with a closed 'ô' sound (e.g. "dono", which means "owner"), or with a sound identical to the letter U ('ooh') (e.g. "excesso", which means "excess"), which happens when the letter comes up as the last one in the word.

The **letter U**, just as the letter I, never changes its pronunciation. It is always read with an 'ooh' sound (e.g. "uva", which means "grape").

1.1.2 Consonants

The **letter H** has no sound when it's used as the first letter of a word. But if combined with other consonants in the middle of words, it produces specific sounds. More about this in sub-section *1.1.3 Combinations*.

The **letter K** has the same sound as in English. As a matter of fact, it is only used in words that have foreign origin (e.g. "ketchup", "kung fu", and "kamikaze").

The **letter L** has a particularity about it in terms of its pronunciation. In Brazilian Portuguese, when it appears at the end of a word, it is read with a 'w' sound (e.g. "papel", which means "paper"). In the middle of the word however, it maintains its original 'el' sound. In European Portuguese, the letter L is always pronounced the same way, with the 'el' sound.

The **letter R** may have two different sounds. If the letter shows up as the first one in a word (e.g. "rato" which means "mouse") or doubled in the middle (e.g. "carro", which means "car"), it should be pronounced as hard 'rr' sound (as if you were trying to scratch your throat). If it shows up alone in the middle of a word (e.g. "caro", which means "expensive") or at the end of one (e.g. "dólar", which means "dollar"), then it should be pronounced as a rolled R sound. The standard English pronunciation of the letter R is never used in Portuguese, with the exception of a few regional accents.

Examples:

1 - "Rússia" (Russia)

2 - "sorriso" (smile)

3 - "vermelho" (red)

In 1 and 2 there is that hard 'rr' sound whereas in 3 we must use the rolled R sound.

The **letter S** may have two different sounds as well. If it is used as the first letter in a word (e.g. "sorte", which means "luck") then it has a strong 's' sound, like the one in the word snake. However, if it's placed between two vowels it changes to a 'z' sound (e.g. "caso", which means "case"). This 'z' sound doesn't happen if the letter S is between a consonant and a vowel.

The **letter W** can also assume two different sounds: the normal 'w' sound as in English, used almost all the time, or a 'v' sound used in cases such as "kiwi" which is widely read as 'kivi' or proper names such as Wagner, often read as 'Vagner'.

The **letter X** may have four different sounds:

a 'sh' sound as in the word "peixe" (meaning "fish"); it should be read as the 'sh' in the word "show";

a 'cs' sound as in the word "táxi" (meaning "taxi"); it should be read with the same sound as the word in English;

a 'z' sound as in the word "exemplo" (meaning "example"); it should be read as the S in the word "easy";

a 'ss' sound as in the word "próximo" (meaning "next"); it should be read as the S in the word "sing".

Finally, the **letter Y** has the same sound as in English, and it's only used in words with foreign origin (e.g. "yuppie" and "yang").

1.1.3 Combinations

The consonants may also present different pronunciations depending on how they're combined.

The **letter C** may have an 's' sound, as in the English word "race", or a 'k' sound as in the English word "call". The first sound is obtained when you combine the letter C with the letters E or I, while the second sound comes as the result of the combination between the consonant and the letters A, O or U.

Examples:

C + A = 'k' sound – "capacidade" (capacity)

C + E = 's' sound – "acelerado" (accelerated)

C + I = 's' sound – "sociedade" (society)

C + O = 'k' sound – "computador" (computer)

C + U = 'k' sound – "obscuro" (obscure)

This is when the **letter Ç** comes in handy, once it allows to obtain the 's' sound through its insertion before A, O or U.

Examples:

Ç + A = 's' sound – "preguiça" (laziness)

Ç + O = 's' sound – "preço" (price)

Ç + U = 's' sound – "açúcar" (sugar)

Note that there's no 'çe' or 'çi' in Portuguese because that is simply not necessary.

The **letter G** may have a soft 'gee' sound, as in the English word "beige", or a dry 'g' sound as in the English word "girl". It depends on the vowel you're combining it with. The rule is very similar to the one used for the letter C.

Examples:

G + A = dry 'g' sound – "<u>ga</u>solina" (gasoline)

G + E = soft 'g' sound – "<u>ge</u>lo" (ice)

G + I = soft 'g' sound – "<u>ges</u>so" (plaster)

G + O = dry 'g' sound – "A<u>go</u>sto" (August)

G + U = dry 'g' sound – "a<u>gu</u>do" (acute)

In order to obtain the dry 'g' sound for E and I, you can combine the letter G with the letter U.

Examples:

G + U + E = 'gge' sound – "hambur<u>gue</u>r" (hamburger)

G + U + I = 'ggi' sound – "<u>gui</u>tarra" (guitar)

The **letter H** can be combined with other consonants originating either one of three digraphs: 'ch', 'lh', or 'nh'. A digraph is a sound that is originated through the combination of two different letters.

Examples:

C + H = 'sh' sound – "<u>ch</u>eio" (full)

L + H = 'lli' sound, as in the word "mi<u>lli</u>on", but spoken very fast – "a<u>lh</u>o" (garlic)

N + H = special 'ñ' sound, as in the word "lasa<u>gna</u>" – "so<u>nh</u>o" (dream)

The **letter Q** is always used in combination with the letter U, which is placed right after it, to create a 'k' sound before any vowel.

Examples:

Q + U + A = 'kua' sound – "<u>qua</u>lidade" (quality)

Q + U + E = 'ke' sound – "almanaque" (almanac); in some cases the U is read as well, creating a 'kue' sound – "consequência" (consequence)

Q + U + I = 'ki' sound – "anarquia" (anarchy); in some cases the U is read as well, creating a 'kui' sound – "liquidação" (liquidation)

Q + U + O = 'kuo' sound – "quociente" (quocient)

Note that 'quu' does not exist. The 'ku' sound is already obtained by writing 'cu' as seen above.

1.2 Accentuation

Accents can change the pronunciation of letters quite a lot. It's very important that you know about them and learn to distinguish between them.

1.2.1 Acute accent

The acute accent (´) is the most common one in Portuguese. It can be used in all vowels.

In **letter A**, you can find it in words such as:

Água [ah-gua] – Water

Armário [ar-mah-ree-oo] – Closet

Sandália [son-dah-lee-ah] – Sandália

The acute accent in the letter A gives it an open 'ah' sound.

In **letter E**, it is used in words such as:

Régua [r(y)eah-goo-ah] – Ruler

Média [m(y)eah-dee-ah] – Average

Espécie [es-p(y)eah-see] – Species

Again, the acute accent gives the letter E an open '(y)eah' sound.

In **letter I**, it is used in words such as:

Índio [in-dee-oo] – Indian

Promíscuo [pro-mis-cwoo] – Promíscuo

Possível [poo-see-vel] – Possible

In **letter O**, it is used in words such as:

Óleo [aw-lee-oo] – Oil

Código [caw-dee-goo] – Code

Ótimo [aw-tee-moo] – Great

The acute accent also gives the letter O an open 'aw' sound.

In **letter U**, it is used in words such as:

Útil [oo-teel] – Useful

Último [ool-tee-moo] – Last

Refúgio [reh-foo-gee-oo] – Refúgio

1.2.2 Grave accent

The grave accent (`) is used much less, and it only applies to the letter A. Very few words use them and all of them result from the contraction of the preposition "a" with a certain pronoun: à, às, àquele, àqueles, àquela, àquelas, àquilo (to the / to those / to that). More about them in *Chapter 3 – Pronouns* and *Chapter 5 – Prepositions*, respectively. See below some examples and their pronunciation.

À [ah] – To the

Àqueles [ah-ka(y)-la(y)] – To those

Àquilo [ah-kee-loo] – To that

1.2.3 Circumflex accent

The circumflex accent (^) can be used in the letters A, E, and O and it closes the sound of those vowels.

In **letter A**, it is used in words such as:

Câmara [cuh-muh-ruh] – Cham

Crânio [cruh-nee-oo] – Crane

Ângulo [un-goo-loo] – Angle

The circumflex accent in the letter A gives it a closed 'uh' sound.

In **letter E**, it is used in words such as:

Mês [ma(y)sh] – Month

Fêmea [fa(y)-mee-uh] – Female

Inglês [in-gla(y)sh] – English

Again, the circumflex accent gives the letter E a closed 'a(y)' sound.

In **letter O**, it is used in words such as:

Estômago [es-tô-muh-goo] – Stomach

Avô [ah-vô] – Grandfather

Fôlego [fô-la(y)-goo] – Breath

The circumflex accent also gives the letter O a closed 'ô' sound, as in Brigitte Bardot's name.

1.2.4 Tilde

The tilde accent (~) can be used in letters A and O. It indicates a nasal sound.

In **letter A**, it is used in words such as:

Maçã [muh-so(n)] – Apple

Botão [Boo-tâu] – Button

Balão [Buh-lâu] – Balloon

In **letter O**, it is used in words such as:

Opções [op-soys] – Options

Emoções [ee-moo-soys] – Emotions

Ladrões [lah-droys] - Thieves

With the letter O, it's used usually in "-ões" terminations, to form the plural of words with "-ão" terminations (the examples above represent the plural of the words "opção", "emoção", and "ladrão", respectively), or in certain conjugations of 2ⁿᵈ conjugation verbs terminated in "-or" (e.g. the verb "supor", meaning "to suppose", features the conjugated forms "supõem" or "supõe"). To see more about the formation of plurals, check section *1.4 Singular and plural*.

1.2.5 Cedilla

The cedilla (,) is only applied to the letter C, becoming Ç and thus changing its pronunciation to an 's' sound. It's the only accent that is written below the letter and it's used before the vowels A, O and U.

Examples:

Cabeça [kuh-ba(y-suh] – Head

Caroço [kuh-rô-soo] – Seed

Coração [kuh-rô-soo] – Heart

Doçura [dô-soo-ruh] – Sweetness

1.2.6 Hyphen

The hyphen (-) is used in compound words (see section *1.3 Nouns and articles*).

Examples:

Guarda-chuva [goo-ar-duh-shoo-vuh] – Umbrella

Arco-íris [ar-koo-ee-reesh] – Rainbow

Algodão-doce [al-goo-dâu-dô-suh] – Cotton candy

Guarda-costas [gooar-duh-kaws-tuhsh] – Bodyguard

1.3 Nouns and articles

Nouns can belong to several different categories. They can be proper, common, collective, simple, compound, masculine and / or feminine. Let's get into that.

Proper nouns refer to people, places, names, etc. They're always written with capital first letter (e.g. Maria, Lisboa, Deus…).

Common nous are every other words that don't fit into the proper nouns category, so they refer to most words in the Portuguese language (e.g. microondas, bicicleta, caneca, commando, fevereiro…).

Collective nouns are the ones that refer to a group of things from the same kind.

Examples:

Elenco [ee-len-koo] – Cast (collective of actors)

Ninhada [nee-ñah-duh] – Litter (collective of newborn animals)

Rebanho [re-buh-ñoo] – Herd (collective of animals / mammals)

Enxame [en-shuh-me] – Swarm (collective of flying insects)

Quadrilha [kua-dree-llia] – Gang (collective of criminals)

Alcateia [al-kuh-tay-ah] – Pack (collective of wolves)

Coro [kô-roo] – Choir (collective of singers)

Multidão [mool-tee-dâu] – Crowd (colective of people)

Mata [mah-tuh] – Wood (collective of trees)

Cardume [kur-doo-me] – Shoal (collective of fish)

Simple nouns possess only one radical.

Examples:

Sol [sol] – Sun

Flor [flôr] – Flower

Árvore [ar-voo-re] – Tree

Nuvem [noo-vein] – Cloud

Compound nouns possess two different radicals and they may or may not be separated by a hyphen.

Examples:

Girassol [gee-ruh-sol] – Sunflower

Beija-flor [bay-juh-flôr] – Hummingbird

Guarda-chuva [goo-ar-duh-shoo-vuh] – Umbrella

Passatempo [pah-suh-tem-poo] – Hobby

Note that "girassol" and "passatempo" don't have a hyphen. The result from the combination of different words.

Girassol = gira (spin) + sol (sun); Passatempo = passa (spends) + tempo (time)

Masculine nouns are the ones that can be preceded by the articles "o" or "os".

Feminine nouns are the nouns that can be preceded by the articles "a" or "as".

Every noun in Portuguese is either masculine or feminine. However, when we're talking about places, for example, a lot of the times it is accepted to refer to some of them as if they were gender neutral. More about this in *Chapter 8 – Useful expressions and vocabulary*.

Articles, or **artigos** in Portuguese, are words that appear before the noun and that always agree to it in number (singular or plural) and gender (masculine or feminine).

The articles that indicate a specific noun are called **artigos definidos** (defined articles), since when someone uses them there's no doubt about the object that is being referred. Those can be "o", "a", "os", or "as":

"o" – defined article, masculine and singular (e.g. "**O** computador é meu." – "The computer is mine.")

"a" – defined article, feminine and singular (e.g. "Eu trouxe **a** minha mochila. – I brought my backpack.")

"os" – defined article, masculine and plural (e.g. "Conheci ontem **os** pais da Marta. – Yesterday I have met Marta's parents.")

"as" – defined article, feminine and plural (e.g. "Já marquei **as** minhas férias. – I have already set my vacations.")

All of these defined articles meet their English equivalent in the word "the". Note that in the second example, with "os pais" meaning "parents", the masculine article is used even though we're referring to a man and a woman. In a mixed environment, the masculine plural form should always be used.

The articles that precede unspecified nouns are called **artigos indefinidos** (undefined articles), and they also vary in gender and number. They can be "um", "uma", "uns", or "umas":

"um" – undefined article, masculine and singular (e.g. "**Um** dia chegarei lá. – Someday I will get there.")

"uma" – undefined article, feminine and singular (e.g. "Vi hoje **uma** mulher parecida contigo. – Today I've seen a woman that looked like you.")

"uns" – undefined article, masculine and plural (e.g. "**Uns** são piores do que outros – Some are worse than others.")

"umas" – undefined article, feminine and plural (e.g. "Comprei várias laranjas: **umas** estavam boas, outras estavam podres. – I bought several oranges: some were good, some were rotten.")

Note that in every example showed above there is no way of knowing for sure who or what is the object that is being mentioned. The English equivalent for these articles would be the words "some" and "a".

1.4 Singular and plural

In Portuguese the formation of the plural form can assume different configurations, depending on the termination of the singular noun. Below, you can see how to form the plural of several types of words, depending on their terminations:

'-O' (Rato); '-OS' (Ratos)

'-A' (Janela); '-AS' (Janelas)

'-ÃO' (Cidadão); '-ÃOS' (Cidadãos)

'-ÃO' (Limão); '-ÕES' (Limões)

'-ÃO' (Alemão); '-ÃES' (Alemães)

'-Ã' (Anã); '-ÃS' (Anãs)

'-EL' (Papel); '-EIS' (Papeis)

'-AL' (Jornal); '-AIS' (Jornais)

'-R' (Lugar); '-RES' (Lugares)

'-ÓI' (Herói); '-ÓIS' (Heróis)

'-ÕE' (Põe); '-ÕEM' (Põem)

'-AGEM' (Garagem); '-AGENS' (Garagens)

'-Z' (Capaz); '-ZES' (Capazes)

'-OL' (Anzol); '-ÓIS' (Anzóis)

'-UL' (Azul); '-UIS' (Azuis)

'-IL'[1] (Funil); '-IS' (Funis)

'-IL'[2] (Útil); '-EIS' (Úteis)

'-X' (Tórax); '-X' (Tórax)

The nouns above mean "mouse", "window", "citizen", "lemon", "German", "midget", "paper", "newspaper", "place", "hero", "(he) puts", "garage", "capable", "fishing hook", "blue", "funnel", "useful", and "thorax", respectively.

You can notice the words that end in '-o' and '-a' form the plural though the insertion of the letter S at the end of it. The same thing happens for '-ã' and '-ói' terminations. The '-ão' termination admits three different plurals. There is no specific rule implied. Regarding any termination consisting of a vowel and the letter L, the plural is formed by dropping the L and replacing it by '-is' at the end. However, there is a special case concerning the '-il' termination.

[1] '-il' can transform into '-is' if the word's tonic syllable is the last one;

[2] '-il' transforms into '-eis' when the tonic syllable is the second to last one.

1.5 Masculine and feminine

In Portuguese language the subject "it" doesn't exist. Everything is either masculine or feminine, even objects and animals.

Even though this doesn't work all the time, you can assume as a rule of thumb that words ending with '-a' or '-as' are feminine; whereas words ending with '-o' or '-os' are masculine. Words ending with '-ão' can be either masculine or feminine. Usually, words ending with '-dade' or '-gem' are feminine.

Examples:

(o) Livro [lee-vroo] – Book

(as) Cadeiras [kuh-day-rus] – Chairs

(a) Casa [kah-zuh] – House

(o) Papel [puh-pell] – Paper

(a) Cidade [see-dah-duh] – City

(a) Garagem [guh-rah-gem] – Garage

So, how to transform a masculine noun into a feminine one? Check below to see how it works for the most common terminations:

'-O' (Médico); '-A' (Médica)

'-R' (Doutor); '-RA' (Doutora)

'-ÃO' (Artesão); '-Ã' (Artesã)

'-ÃO' (Valentão); '-ONA' (Valentona)

'-E' (Agente); '-E' (Agente)

'-ISTA' (Dentista); '-ISTA' (Dentista)

The words above mean "physician", "doctor", "craftsman", "bully boy" (slang), "agent", and "dentist". The '-ão' termination is normally transformed into the feminine form through '-ã'. However, in most slang words is very common to use the '-ona' termination instead.

1.6 The sentence

Putting together a sentence is very important when you're trying to communicate. In this section, we'll see the basic aspects of a sentence and how to build different types of sentences.

1.6.1 Structuring a sentence

Every sentence must have a subject and a predicate. The subject is the person or object the sentence is about; the predicate says something about the subject.

Examples:

1 - As praias estão muito poluídas. (The beaches are very polluted.)

2 - A Sofia comprou uma barra de chocolate. (Sofia bought a chocolate bar.)

In the first sentence, the subject is "As praias" ("The beaches"); in the second sentence the subject is "A Sofia" ("Sofia"). Everything else after that is the predicate.

The predicate consists mainly of the verb and the complements, which can be direct or indirect ones.

The verb informs about what is happening; the complements complete the sentence and usually involve a preposition.

Again, looking at the examples above, we have for the **first sentence**:

Subject: As praias

Predicate: estão muito poluídas.

Dismembering the predicate:

Verb: estão (conjugation of the verb "estar")

Complements: muito poluídas.

In the **second sentence**:

Subject: A Sofia

Predicate: comprou uma barra de chocolate.

Dismembering the predicate:

Verb: comprou (conjugation of the verb "comprar")

Complements: uma barra de chocolate.

1.6.2 Forms of sentences

Sentences can be either affirmative or negative. As the name suggests, a sentence is affirmative when a positive affirmation is being made, while a negative sentence uses the negative form in it.

Examples of affirmative sentences:

Ontem eu fui ao dentista. (Yesterday I went to the dentist.)

Aquele vidro está muito sujo. (That glass is very dirty.)

Eu fui contratado por aquela empresa. (I was hired by that company.)

O meu pai está em casa. (My dad is home.)

To form a negative sentence in Portuguese you should place the word "no" or another adverb of negation (more about this in *Chapter 2 – Adverbs*) before the verb you want to deny, whether it is the main verb or the auxiliary verb.

Examples of negative sentences:

Ontem eu não fui ao dentista. (Yesterday I didn't go to the dentist.)

Aquele vidro nem está muito sujo. (That glass is not very dirty.)

Eu jamais seria contratado por aquela empresa. (I would never be hired by that company.)

O meu pai nunca está em casa. (My dad is never home.)

1.6.3 Types of sentences

Any sentence, affirmative or negative, can be grouped in one of seven different categories.

Frases declarativas (Declarative sentences)

They intend to communicate a fact or simply to state something, and they always end with a period.

Examples:

O meu irmão foi ao cinema. (My brother went to the movies.)

Eu costumo estacionar sempre no mesmo lugar. (I normally park always on the same spot.)

Não sei se vou poder ir. (I'm not sure if I'm going to make it.)

Frases interrogativas (Interrogative sentences)

They occur when a question is asked, and they always ends with a question mark. The question can be direct (sentence 1) or indirect (sentence 2).

Examples:

1 – Vocês estão com frio? (Are you feeling cold?)

2 – Gostaria de saber se vocês estão com frio. (I would like to know if you're feeling cold.)

Both of these are affirmative interrogative sentences. Let's see examples of negative affirmative sentences:

3 – Ele não ouviu o que eu disse? (Didn't he hear what I said?)

4 – Tu e o teu irmão ainda não estão prontos? (You and your brother are not ready yet?)

Frases imperativas (Imperative sentences)

They determine an order, an advice, or a request. They can end with a period mark or with an exclamation mark.

Examples:

Chama a tua mãe! (Call your mother!)

Não faças isso! (Don't do that!)

Vá até lá e pergunte. (Go over there and ask.)

Frases exclamativas (Exclamatory sentences)

In these sentences, the speaker expresses an emotional state. They always end with an exclamation mark.

Examples:

Que lindo dia! (What a beautiful day!)

Bela casa! (Nice house!)

Aquele filme foi péssimo! (That movie sucked!)

Besides the types of sentences we have just seen, they can also be classified as nominal sentences or verbal sentences.

Nominal sentences, or **frases nominais** in Portuguese, don't have any verb. Some examples from the sentences above:

Que lindo dia! (What a beautiful day!)

Bela casa! (Nice house!)

Verbal sentences, or **frases verbais** in Portuguese, are the most common type and they must have a verb. Again, some examples from the sentences above:

<u>Chama</u> a tua mãe! (<u>Call</u> your mother!)

O meu irmão <u>foi</u> ao cinema. (My brother <u>went</u> to the movies.)

Chapter 2 – Adverbs

Adverbs can change the meaning of a sentence, by modifying the verb, adjective, adverb, etc. They split into several categories, according to the circumstances they refer to. The list is extensive but check below some of the most common examples for each category.

2.1 Adverbs of time

Quando (When)

Ontem (Yesterday)

Hoje (Today)

Amanhã (Tomorrow)

Antes (Before)

Depois (After)

Sempre (Always)

Nunca (Never)

Jamais (Never)

Cedo (Early)

Tarde (Late)

Já (Already)

Agora (Now)

Ora (Now)

Depois (Later)

Logo (Soon)

Ainda (Yet)

Examples:

O João chegou <u>agora</u> da fábrica. (João has just arrived from the factory.)

<u>Amanhã</u> viajaremos para a Alemanha. (Tomorrow we'll travel to Germany.)

Vem <u>já</u> para casa! (Come home right now!)

2.2 Adverbs of place

Onde (Where)

Aqui (Here)

Aí (There)

Ali (There)

Além (Beyond)

Lá (Over there)

Acima (Above)

Abaixo (Below)

Aquém[1]

Dentro (Inside)

Fora (Outside)

Diante (Before[2])

Defronte (In front of)

Atrás (Behind)

Longe (Far)

Perto (Close)

[1] Means the opposite of "Além" ("Beyond"), and does not have a direct English translation.

[2] With a meaning of place, as in "She was standing before her parents."

Examples:

A Maria mora perto do tribunal. (Maria lives near the courthouse.)

Deixei o carro fora de garagem. (I left the car outside the garage.)

A quinta fica além daquelas montanhas. (The farm is beyond those mountains.)

2.3 Adverbs of quantity

Quão (How)

Assaz (Rather)

Bastante (Quite)

Muito (Much)

Pouco (Little)

Quase (Almost)

Tanto (Somewhat)

Tão (Such a)

Mais (More)

Menos (Less)

Apenas (Only)

Nada (Nothing)

Ele pareceu-me ser um rapaz <u>assaz</u> inteligente. (He seemed to me like a rather intelligent boy.)

Hoje levo <u>apenas</u> o necessário. (Today I'm taking only the necessary.)

Devias usar <u>menos</u> açúcar. (You should use less sugar.)

2.4 Adverbs of mode

Como (Like)

Assim (That way)

Bem (Well)

Mal (Badly)

Também (Also)

Devagar (Slowly)

Melhor (Better)

Pior (Worse)

Rapidamente (Quickly)

Provavelmente (Probably)

Certamente (Certainly)

Inteligentemente (Brightly)

Examples:

Notei <u>rapidamente</u> que algo estava errado. (I quickly spotted something was wrong.)

Estou <u>bem</u>, obrigado. (I'm fine, thank you.)

É melhor irmos <u>devagar</u> para não nos perdermos. (We better go slowly so we don't get lost.)

It's possible to form an infinity of mode adverbs ending with "-mente". All you have to do is to add that termination to the feminine form of an adjective:

Sábia (wise) + "-mente" = Sabiamente (wisely)

Humilde (humble) + "-mente" = Humildemente (humbly)

Calma (calm) + "-mente" = Calmamente (calmly)

2.5 Adverbs of affirmation

Sim (Yes)

Seguramente (Surely)

Efetivamente (In effect)

Example:

Efetivamente, confirmou-se essa informação. (In effect, that information was confirmed.)

2.6 Adverbs of negation

Não (No)

Nunca (Never)

Jamais (Never)

Nem (Nor)

Example:

Nunca tinha visto algo assim! (I had never seen something like this before!)

2.7 Adverbs of doubt

Talvez (Maybe)

Porventura (By chance)

Quiçá (Perhaps)

Possivelmente (Possibly)

<u>Example</u>:

Se porventura encontrar as minhas chaves, por favor avise-me. (If you find my keys by chance, please let me know.)

2.8 Adverbs of demonstration or designation

Eis (These are / here they are)

Ei (This is / here it is)

<u>Example</u>:

<u>Eis</u> os meus quadros! (Here they are, my paintings!)

Chapter 3 – Pronouns

Pronouns, or **pronomes** in Portuguese, are the words that join or replace the nouns, and they can belong to six different categories: personal, possessive, demonstrative, relative, interrogative, and indefinite.

3.1 Personal pronouns

Personal pronouns, or **pronomes pessoais** in Portuguese, are the words that indicate who the people are in a sentence. They can be divided into three sub-categories: pronomes pessoais retos (straight personal pronouns), pronomes pessoais oblíquos átonos (unstressed oblique personal pronouns), and pronomes pessoais oblíquos tónicos (stressed oblique personal pronouns). Don't worry too much about the names, the important thing is to understand in which situations they should be used.

3.1.1 Straight personal pronouns

They indicate who is the subject of a sentence. These are the personal pronouns used for conjugating verbs.

When conjugating the verbs, you'll find six different personal pronouns:

Singular

1st person – Eu (I)

2nd person – Tu (You)

3rd person – Ele / Ela (He / She / It)[1][2]

<u>Plural</u>

1st person – Nós (We)

2nd person – Vós (You)

3rd person – Eles / Elas (They)

[1] Note that there's no word in Portuguese for "it". As mentioned before, every object, animal or person has to be either masculine or feminine.

[2] When we refer to the second person of the singular form, speakers of European Portuguese commonly use the "Tu" pronoun, and the pronoun "Você" if talking to strangers or on formal occasions, omitting the pronoun on this last case and just using the conjugated verb tense. "Você" is not normally listed in any pronoun list or conjugation table since it's considered by many to be a grammatically incorrect colloquialism. In Brazilian Portuguese however, "Tu" is very rarely used. Instead, Brazilians use the personal pronoun "Você" all the time, in every occasion. When referring to the second person of the plural form, both European and Brazilian Portuguese speakers use the pronoun "Vocês", even though Portuguese people may eventually use the more formal "Vós" pronoun.

Just like we have previously discussed in *Chapter 1, section 1.3* when discussing articles, in pronouns the masculine plural form always prevails in a mixed environment, i.e., when we're referring to men and women simultaneously. For example, in a school class with boys and girls the teacher would refer to the group of his/her students by using the pronoun "eles". Obviously, the same thing would happen if the class was all boys. So the only situation in which you would use "elas" is if you're referring to a group that features exclusively women and/or feminine nouns.

3.1.2 Unstressed oblique personal pronouns

<u>Singular</u>

1st person – Me

2nd person – Te

3rd person – O, a, lhe, se

<u>Plural</u>

1st person – Nos

2nd person – Vos

3rd person – Os, as, lhes, se

These pronouns possess a different function in a sentence. When they're used, they don't indicate the subject of the sentence, they indicate the person / people who the action had an effect on. They always appear connected to the verb, before or after it.

<u>Examples</u>:

Eu enganei-<u>me</u>. (I was wrong. – translates literally to 'I mistook myself'): Who did I mistake? Myself. ("me")

Eu <u>te</u> avisei (I warned you): Who did I warn? You. ("te")

O João foi embora cedo. Ninguém o viu sair. (João left early. Nobody saw him leave.): Who did nobody see? João. ("o")

Eles nos disseram que estava tudo bem. (They told us everything was fine): Who did they tell? Us. ("nos").

3.1.3 Stressed oblique personal pronouns

<u>Singular</u>

1st person – Mim, comigo

2nd person – Ti, contigo

3rd person – Si, ele, ela, consigo

Plural

1st person – Nós, conosco

2nd person – Vós, convosco

3rd person – Si, eles, elas, consigo

Stressed oblique personal pronouns always appear next to a preposition. See the following examples:

Queres vir comigo? (Do you want to come with me?)

Faça o que for melhor para si. (Do what's best for you.)

Eu não estou contra eles. (I'm not against them.)

Pensei que o tinha deixado contigo. (I thought I had left it with you.)

The words "comigo", "contigo", "consigo", "conosco", "convosco" were created from the combination of the preposition "com" ("with") and the personal pronouns "mim", "ti", "si", "nós", and "vós", respectively.

3.2 Possessive pronouns

Possessive pronouns, or **pronomes possessivos** in Portuguese, are the words which indicate that something belongs to a certain individual. Since pronouns vary in number and gender, there are a total of 24 pronouns. Below you can see the four different possessive pronouns that exist for each personal pronoun. Next to the personal pronoun are presented (in order): masculine singular, feminine singular, masculine plural, and feminine plural.

Eu – meu, minha, meus, minhas (my / mine)

Tu – teu, tua, teus, tuas (your / yours)

Ele / Ela – seu, sua, seus, suas[1] (his; her / hers, its)

Nós – nosso, nossa, nossos, nossas (our / ours)

Vós – vosso, vossa, vossos, vossas (your / yours)

Eles / Elas – seu, sua, seus, suas (their / theirs)

[1] On daily conversations, very rarely people use "seu", "sua", "seus" or "suas" when referring to the third person either singular or plural. People normally adopt the possessive pronouns "dele" or "dela" (3rd person singular) and "deles" or "delas" (3rd person plural). In these cases, the possessive pronoun should always appear after the object or instead of it, never before.

Examples:

Não há dúvidas, a culpa foi dele. (There is no doubt, it was his fault.)

A Sara foi andar de bicicleta, mas a mãe dela está em casa. (Sara went for a bike ride but her mom is home.)

So how do "você" and "vocês" work in this case? The personal pronoun "Você", often used in Brazilian Portuguese, uses the same possessive pronouns as "Ele". For example: "Você sabe onde deixou o seu relógio?" ("Do you know where you left your watch?").

When referring to the second person of the plural form, things vary in European and Brazilian Portuguese. Portuguese people use "vosso", "vossa", "vossos", and "vossas" therefore following the table above. Brazilians, on the other hand, usually replace those four possessive pronouns in daily conversations by the phrase "de vocês", which always comes after the object.

Examples:

Este carro é meu. (This car is mine.) 1st person singular

(European Portuguese) O teu filho já saiu. (Your son has already left.) 2nd person singular

(Brazilian Portuguese) O seu filho já saiu. (Your son has already left.) 2nd person singular

As <u>nossas</u> casas têm a mesma cor (<u>Our</u> houses have the same color.) 1st person plural

(European Portuguese) A <u>vossa</u> turma é a melhor da escola. Vocês deveriam estar orgulhosos. (<u>Your</u> class is the best of the school. You should be proud.) 2nd person plural

(Brazilian Portuguese) A turma <u>de vocês</u> é a melhor da escola. Vocês deveriam estar orgulhosos. (<u>Your</u> class is the best of the school. You should be proud.) 2nd person plural

3.3 Demonstrative pronouns

Demonstrative pronouns, or **pronomes demonstrativos** in Portuguese, serve to demonstrate the position of a certain entity in relation to the person who is speaking. They can be 1st person demonstrative pronouns, 2nd person demonstrative pronouns or 3rd person demonstrative pronouns.

<u>1st person demonstrative pronouns</u> refer to something that is close or that is positioned near the person who is speaking.

Este – Masculine singular (e.g. "<u>Este</u> é o meu pai. – <u>This</u> is my father.")

Esta – Feminine singular (e.g. "Tens uma caneta igual a <u>esta</u>? – Do you have a pen like <u>this</u>?")

Estes – Masculine plural (e.g. "São <u>estes</u> os teus fones? – Are <u>these</u> your headphones?")

Estas – Feminine plural (e.g. "<u>Estas</u> foram as melhores férias que eu já tive. – <u>These</u> were the best vacations I've ever had.")

Isto – This pronoun is not defined neither in gender or number. It can be used in two different situations:

When you don't know what you're looking at and therefore you cannot attribute a gender to it (e.g. "O que é <u>isto</u>? – What is <u>this</u>?").

Or in a derogatory way, when you want to depreciate something (e.g. "Achas mesmo que isto serve para alguma coisa? – Do you really think this serves any purpose?")

2nd person demonstrative pronouns refer to something that is close or that is positioned near the listener of the person who is speaking.

Esse – Masculine singular (e.g. "Não vi nenhum carro igual a esse – I haven't seen any car like that")

Essa – Feminine singular (e.g. "Infelizmente, não tenho vagas para essa semana – Unfortunately, I don't have any openings for that week.")

Esses – Masculine plural (e.g. "Já tinha visto alguns tablets como esses. – I had already seen some tablets like those.")

Essas – Feminine plural (e.g. "Essas moedas não vão chegar. – Those coins won't be enough.")

Isso – This pronoun is not defined neither in gender or number. Like "Isso", it can be used under the same circumstances defined for that pronoun. (e.g. "Larga isso e vem aqui. – Drop that and come here.")

3rd person demonstrative pronouns refer to something that is more distant or positioned further both from the person who is speaking and from the listener as well.

Aquele – Masculine singular (e.g. "Aquele senhor esteve aqui na semana passada. – That gentleman was here last week.")

Aquela – Feminine singular (e.g. "Viste aquela mensagem que te enviei? – Did you see that message I sent you?")

Aqueles – Masculine plural (e.g. "Não quero voltar para aqueles lugares. – I don't wanna go back to those places.")

Aquelas – Feminine plural (e.g. "Podes buscar aquelas caixas ali em cima? – Can you get those boxes up there?"

Aquilo – This pronoun is not defined neither in gender or number. Like "Isso" and "Isto", it can be used under the same circumstances defined for that pronoun. (e.g. "<u>Aquilo</u> foi horrível. – <u>That</u> was awful.")

3.4 Relative pronouns

Relative pronouns, or **pronomes relativos** in Portuguese, refer to an object that was previously mentioned in the same sentence (e.g. "Chegou o livro que tinhas encomendado – The book that you ordered has arrived.")

O qual, a qual, os quais, as quais (which)

Cujo, cuja, cujos, cujas (whose)

Quanto, quanta, quantos, quantas (much)

Que, quem, onde (that, who, where)

Note that the first three lines feature relative pronouns that vary in gender and number. What we have is (by order): the masculine singular, the feminine singular, the masculine plural, and the feminine plural. In the last line, we find relative pronouns that don't vary in gender nor in number, and for that reasons they're called invariáveis (invariable).

Examples:

Não sei o que ele está a querer dizer. (I don't know what he is trying to say.)

Na segunda-feira visitei a casa da minha tia, a qual era enorme. (On Monday I visited my aunt's house, which was huge.)

O edifício cujas paredes foram pintadas está ali. (The building whose walls were painted is over there.)

Compra tanto quanto for preciso. (Buy as much as necessary.)

3.5 Interrogative pronouns

Interrogative pronouns, or **pronomes interrogativos** in Portuguese, are those used in questions but always referring to the 3rd person (e.g. "Ele perguntou quem tinha feito aquilo. – He asked who had done that.")

Quanto, quanta, quantos, quantas (how many)

Qual, quais (which)

Que (that; which)

Quem (who)

3.6 Indefinite pronouns

Indefinite pronouns, or **pronomes indefinidos** in Portuguese, are those who refer to the 3rd person in the speech but in a generic sense (e.g. "Alguém entrou no jardim. – Someone has entered the garden.)

Muito, muita, muitos, muitas (many)

Pouco, pouca, poucos, poucas (few)

Tanto, tanta, tantos, tantas (so many)

Todo, toda, todos, todas (all; everyone)

Tudo (everything; all)

Nada (nothing; anything)

Cada (each)

Um, uma, uns, umas (some)

Nenhum, nenhuma, nenhuns, nenhumas (none)

Algum, alguma, alguns, algumas (any)

Alguém (someone)

Ninguém (nobody)

Outro, outra, outros, outras (other, others)

Ambos, ambas (both)

Chapter 4 – Adjectives

Adjectives, or **adjetivos** in Portuguese, are words that express a quality or a certain characteristic regarding a noun, and for that reason they're always connected to it.

4.1 Variation in gender and number

The adjectives that vary in gender assume two different forms, they can be either masculine or feminine. For example, the adjective "engraçado(a)" ("funny").

O Pedro é engraçad<u>o</u>. (Pedro is funny.)

A Daniela é engraçad<u>a</u>. (Daniela is funny.)

When we have a dual gender adjective, the masculine ones always end in "o"; the feminine ones always end in "a".

The adjectives that don't vary in gender are used the same way both for masculine or feminine. For example, the adjective "contente" ("happy"):

O Hugo está <u>contente</u>. (Pedro is happy.)

A Sofia está <u>contente</u>. (Sofia is happy.)

Every adjective that doesn't end in O or A is uniform.

Adjectives may also vary in number. They always have to agree to the noun and can be either singular or plural. For example, the adjective "engraçado(a)", once again.

O Pedro é engraçado. (Pedro is funny.)

Os teus amigos são engraçados. (Your friends are funny.)

As tuas irmãs são engraçadas. (Your sisters are funny.)

Note the adjective "engraçado(a)" varies both in gender and number.

The adjectives that don't vary in number are used the same way both for singular and plural. For example, the adjective "simples" ("simple"):

Ele é muito simples. (He is very simple.)

São pessoas simples. (They are simple people.)

This happens because the adjective "simples" end with the letter S. Every adjective ending with this letter has the same form for singular and plural.

4.2 Degrees of the adjectives

The degree of the adjective establishes a relation between the qualities of an object /person and the qualities of another object /person. There are three degrees of adjectives:

Normal / positive degree, in which no relation is established with another object /person.

Example: O José é rico. (José is rich.)

Comparative degree, in which simple comparisons are established. There are three types of comparative degrees: inferiority, equality and superiority.

Examples:

Comparative degree of inferiority – O José é <u>menos rico do que</u> o Américo. (José is <u>less rich than</u> Américo.)

Comparative degree of equality – O José é <u>tão rico como</u> o Américo. (José is <u>as rich as</u> Américo.)

Comparative degree of superiority – O José é <u>mais rico do que</u> o Américo (José is <u>richer than</u> Américo).

When forming the comparative degrees of inferiority / superiority, there are a couple of exceptions that don't follow the constructions showed above, i.e., menos + (adjective) + do que / mais + (adjective) + do que. The adjectives "bom / mau" and "grande / pequeno" have a specific and different word to express that position of comparative inferiority / superiority:

<u>Adjective</u>; <u>Comparative of inferiority</u>; <u>Comparative of superiority</u>

Bom / Mau (Good / Bad); Pior (Worse); Melhor (Better)

Grande / Pequeno (Big / Small); Menor (Smaller / Shorter); Maior (Bigger / Taller)

<u>Examples</u>:

A Joana teve uma nota <u>pior do que</u> a da Marta. (Joana's grade was <u>worse than</u> Marta's.)

O Artur já se sente <u>melhor do que</u> antes. (Artur is feeling <u>better than</u> he was before.)

A tua prima é <u>menor do que</u> tu. (Your cousin is <u>shorter than</u> you.)

A minha mochila é <u>maior do que</u> isso, não vai caber. (My backpack is <u>bigger than</u> that, it won't fit.)

Then we have the **superlative degree** in which, as the name suggests, superlative statements are made about the qualities of certain person/ object. These can split into four types: superlative relative of inferiority, superlative relative of superiority, superlative absolute analytic / composed, and superlative absolute synthetic /simple.

Examples:

Superlative relative of inferiority – O José é <u>o menos rico</u> de todos os empresários. (José is <u>the less rich</u> among all the entrepreneurs).

Superlative relative of superiority – O José é <u>o mais rico</u> de todos os empresários. (José is <u>the richest</u> out of all the entrepreneurs).

Superlative absolut analitic/composed – O José é <u>muito rico</u>. (José is <u>very rich</u>.)

Superlative absolute synthetic – O José é <u>riquíssimo</u>. (José is <u>super rich</u>.)

Again, when forming the superlative relative degrees of inferiority / superiority, the same adjectives listed before also don't follow these rules.

<u>Adjective</u>; <u>Superlative of inferiority</u>; <u>Superlative of superiority</u>

Bom / Mau (Good / Bad); Pior (Worst); Melhor (Best)

Grande / Pequeno (Big / Small); Menor (Smallest / Shortest); Maior (Biggest / Tallest)

<u>Examples</u>:

Este foi <u>o pior</u> dia de toda a semana. (This was <u>the worst</u> day of the entire week.)

Aquele apartamento foi <u>o melhor</u> que eu consegui encontrar. (That apartment was <u>the best</u> I could find.)

O Bruno é <u>o menor</u> aluno da turma. (Bruno is <u>the smallest</u> student of the class.)

Ele é <u>o melhor</u> profissional da sua área. (He is <u>the best</u> professional in his field.)

Finally, the superlative absolute synthetic is often formed by adding the suffixes "-íssimo" to the radical of the adjective. When the adjective ends with a vowel, occurs the suppression of that vowel.

Examples:

Ágil (Agile) – Agilíssimo

Belo (Beautiful) – Belíssimo

Triste (Sad) – Tristíssimo

Forte (Strong) – Fortíssimo

There are other cases in which this degree is formed in a different way, depending on the termination of the adjectives in normal degree:

'-IL' (Fácil); '-ÍLIMO' (Facílimo)

'-VEL' (Agradável); '-BILÍSSIMO' (Agradabilíssimo)

'-Z' (Feliz); '-CÍSSIMO' (Felicíssimo)

'-M' (Bom); '-NÍSSIMO' (Boníssimo)

'-ÃO' (Cristão); '-ANÍSSIMO' (Cristianíssimo)

The adjectives listed above mean "easy", "pleasant", "happy, "good", and "Christian", respectively.

Some adjectives that don't follow any of these rules are:

Pobre (Poor) – Paupérrimo

Doce (Sweet) – Dulcíssimo

Fiel (Faithful) – Fidelíssimo

Jovem (Young) – Juvenérrimo

Note that the superlative absolute synthetic degree admits variations in gender and number. Therefore, all of the examples presented were masculine and singular. To change them to the feminine form all you have to do is change the final O to A. To put them in plural form, simply add the letter S at the end of the word.

Chapter 5 – Prepositions

Prepositions, or **preposições** in Portuguese, are small words that express a connection between parts of a sentence that depend on each other.

A (To)

Ante (Before)[1]

Após (Next)

Até (Until)

Com (With)

Contra (Against)

Conforme (According)

Consoante (According)

De (Of; From)

Desde (Since)

Durante (During)

Em (In; At)

Entre (Between)

Exceto (Except)

Mediante (Through)

Para[2] (For)

Perante (In front of)

Per (By; Through)

Por (By; Through)

Salvo (Excepting)

Segundo (According)

Sem (Without)

Sob (Under)

Sobre (About; On)

Trás (Behind)

[1] "Before" in the sense of place, not in the sense of time.

[2] On daily conversation "para" is sometimes abbreviated to "pra", with the suppression of the first letter A. However, in written form you should use the correct form "para".

5.1 Contractions with articles

Prepositions can combine with articles (see *Chapter 1, section 1.3*) to form contractions, or **contrações** in Portuguese. The use of these contractions is fundamental, but especially the contractions that result from the combination with defined articles.

Preposition + article = contraction

Through the combination with defined articles come the following contractions:

a + o = ao [aw]

a + a = à [ah]

a + os = aos [ows]

a + as = às [ahs]

de + o = do [doo]

de + a = da [duh]

de + os = dos [doos]

de + as = das [duhs]

em + o = no [noo]

em + a = na [nuh]

em + os = nos [noos]

em + as = nas [nuhs]

por + o = pelo [pê-loo]

por + a = pela [pê-luh]

por + os = pelos [pê-loos]

por + as = pelas [pê-luhs]

Examples:

Ele conseguiu entregar os documentos ao professor? (Did he manage to deliver the documents to the teacher?)

Ontem foi o aniversário do João. (Yesterday it was João's birthday.)

Hoje de manhã estive na casa dele. (This morning I was at his house.)

Vou enviar esta carta pelos correios. (I'm sending this letter through the mail.)

In the first case the contraction "ao" happened due to the usage of the preposition "a" + the article "o" combined. The translation in English makes it easier to understand. Looking at the example, it's just as if "to the" could be transformed into a single word. The same logic applies to every other example:

Ontem foi o aniversário "de + o" João.

Hoje de manhã estive "em + a" casa dele.

Vou enviar esta carta "por + os" correios.

The combination of the prepositions with the articles is only possible when the noun that comes after the article has a defined gender. When that doesn't happen, you should use the preposition by itself.

By the combination with undefined articles come the following contractions:

de + um = dum [doom]

de + uma = duma [doo-muh]

de + uns = duns [doons]

de + umas = dumas [doo-muhs]

em + um = num [noom]

em + uma = numa [noo-muh]

em + uns = nuns [noons]

em + umas = numas [noo-muhs]

Examples:

Vou pagar as todas as contas duma vez. (I'll pay every bill at once.)

Deixei o casaco num lugar qualquer. (I left my coat somewhere.)

In the written form, is also accepted and very common to use the full preposition and article. For example:

Vou pagar todas as contas de uma vez.

Deixei o casaco em um lugar qualquer.

However, in speaking form people will normally use the contractions instead.

Chapter 6 – Verbs

Even though the third person of the singular and plural forms varies in gender, when conjugating verbs the feminine form ("ela") never appears on any table. That's because verbs don't vary in gender and therefore it's not necessary to present that pronoun. For that reason, we'll present only the masculine pronoun in every verb conjugation table you're about to see.

6.1 Conjugations

Verbs in Portuguese can end with either "-ar", "-er", "-ir" or "-or".

Verbs that end with "-ar" are called 1st conjugation verbs:

Andar (to walk)

Gostar (to like)

Chegar (to arrive)

Chamar (to call)

Dar (to give)

Falar (to speak)

Estar (to be – temporary state)

Passar (to pass)

Comprar (to buy)

Perguntar (to ask – a question)

Chamar (to call)

Comprar (to buy)

Entrar (to enter)

Ficar (to stay)

Indicar (to indicate)

Levar (to take)

Mostrar (to show)

Parar (to stop)

Pensar (to think)

Trocar (to switch)

Verbs that end with "-er" or with "-or" are called 2nd conjugation verbs:

Aprender (to learn)

Ter (to have)

Saber (to know)

Dizer (to say)

Pôr (to put)

Entender (to understand)

Perceber (to understand)

Ser (to be – permanent state)

Fazer (to do)

Poder (can)

Acontecer (to happen)

Beber (to drink)

Comer (to eat)

Chover (to rain)

Correr (to run)

Doer (to hurt)

Expor (to expose)

Impor (to impose)

Ver (to see)

Viver (to live)

Verbs that end with "-ir" are called 3rd conjugation verbs:

Sair (to exit)

Vir (to come)

Sentir (to feel)

Servir (to serve)

Fugir (to escape)

Engolir (to swallow)

Sorrir (to smile)

Proibir (to prohibit)

Cair (to fall)

Ouvir (to hear / to listen)

Dormir (to sleep)

Ir (to go)

Transferir (to transfer)

Incluir (to include)

Subir (to go up / to climb)

Pedir (to ask – a favor)

Existir (to exist)

Conduzir (to drive)

Vestir (to dress)

Abrir (to open)

6.2 Verbal modes and verb tenses

There are four verbal modes which can be split into different verbal tenses:

Modo Indicativo (Indicative Mode) – when the action being mentioned is certain and real.

Modo Conjuntivo / BR: Modo Subjuntivo (Conjunctive / Subjunctive Mode) – when the action hasn't been accomplished yet, is hypothetical or unreal. It expresses uncertainty, doubt and / or desire.

Modo Condicional (Conditional Mode) – when the action can only be completed if a certain condition is fulfilled.

Modo Imperativo (Imperative Mode) – when someone expresses an order, a demand, an advice, an invitation, etc.

Besides those, we can also identify three nominal forms:

Infinitivo (Infinitive) – is the mode in which the verb presents itself in its most vague and general sense.

Particípio passado (Past participle) – it represents an action that is over in the present, in the past or in the future.

Gerúndio (Gerund) – Much more used in Brazilian Portuguese. In European Portuguese it is normally replaced by the preposition "a" + "verb in infinitive mode". For example: "I'm singing", would be "Estou cantando" in Brazilian Portuguese or "Estou a cantar" in European Portuguese.

The Indicative Mode comprehends five verbal tenses:

Presente (Present). Used to express a real situation that is taking place at this moment.

Example: Eu <u>ando</u> na bicicleta. (I ride the bike.)

Pretérito Perfeito Simples (Simple Perfect Past). Used to talk about a situation that took place in a time prior to the current one and which is completely done.

Example: Eu <u>andei</u> na bicicleta. (I rode the bike.)

Pretérito Perfeito Composto (Compound Perfect Past). Used to express an action that began in the past and is still happening in the present day.

Example: <u>Tenho andado</u> na bicicleta. (I have been riding the bike.)

The Compound Perfect Past is made by using the auxiliary verb "TER" ("TO HAVE") conjugated in the Present of the Indicative Mode + the Past Participle of the main verb.

Pretérito Imperfeito (Imperfect Past). Used to describe a situation that took place in a time prior to the current one but that isn't completely done.

Example: Eu <u>andava</u> na bicicleta. (I used to ride the bike.)

Pretérito Mais-que-perfeito Simples (Simple More-than-perfect Past). Normally used in formal ways of writing, almost never on colloquial speeches. It is used to talk about actions that took place in a further past than the one depicted in the Past Perfect tense.

Example: Eu <u>andara</u> na bicicleta.

Pretérito Mais-que-perfeito Composto (Compound More-than-perfect Past). Used in the same situation as the previous verb tense.

Example: Eu <u>tinha andado</u> na bicicleta. (I had ridden the bike.)

The Compound More-than-perfect Past is made by using the auxiliary verb "TER" conjugated in the Imperfect Past of the Indicative Mode + the Past Participle of the main verb.

Futuro Simples (Simple Future). Used to announce an action that hasn't happened yet.

Example: Eu <u>andarei</u> na bicicleta. (I will ride the bike.)

Futuro Composto (Compound Future). Used in the same situation as the previous verb tense.

Example: Amanhã por esta hora ele já <u>terá andado</u> na bicicleta. (Tomorrow by this time he will have ridden ride the bike.)

The Compound Future is made by using the auxiliary verb "TER" conjugated in the Simple Future of the Indicative Mode + the Past Participle of the main verb.

The Conjunctive Mode comprehends three verbal tenses:

Presente (Present). Used to express an action that may happen in the present time.

Example: Eu espero que ele <u>ande</u> na bicicleta. (I hope that he rides the bike.)

Pretérito Imperfeito (Imperfect Past). Used to describe an action that could've had happened in the past (Example 1) or to express an idea of condition or desire (Example 2).

Example 1: Eu esperava que ele <u>andasse</u> na bicicleta. (I was hoping that he would ride the bike.)

Example 2: Se ele <u>estivesse</u> cá, andaria na bicicleta. (If he would be here, he would ride the bike.)

Pretérito Perfeito Composto (Compound Perfect Past). Used to express an action that happened in the past and is completely over and which has a connection with another action that has happened or is happening at this moment.

Example: Embora eu já <u>tenha andado</u> na bicicleta, não me lembro se ela é azul ou verde. (Although I have already ridden the bike, I can't remember whether it is blue or green.)

The Compound Perfect Past is made by using the auxiliary verb "TER" ("TO HAVE") conjugated in the Present of the Conjunctive Mode + the Past Participle of the main verb.

Pretérito Mais-que-perfeito Composto (Compound More-than-perfect Past). Used to indicate an action that happened in the past and is completely over and which has a connection with another action that has also happened in the past.

Example: Embora eu já <u>tivesse andado</u> na bicicleta antes, aquela pareceu ser a primeira vez. (Even though I had already ridden the bike before, that seemed like the first time.)

The Compound More-than-perfect Past is made by using the auxiliary verb "TER" conjugated in the Imperfect Pastt of the Conjunctive Mode + the Past Participle of the main verb.

Futuro Simples (Simple Future). Used to express an action that may happen in the future (Example 1) or to express an idea of condition or desire (Example 2).

Example 1: Quando ele <u>estiver</u> aqui, andará na bicicleta. (When he is here, he will ride the bike.)

Example 2: Se ele <u>estiver</u> aqui hoje à tarde, andará na bicicleta. (If he is here this afternoon, he will ride the bike.)

Futuro Composto (Compound Future). Used to indicate a fact that would take place after the present time but before another action that will happen in the future and to which this action is connected.

Example: Quando ele <u>tiver chegado</u>, avisa-me. (Let me know when he arrives.)

The Compound Future is made by using the auxiliary verb "TER" conjugated in the Simple Future of the Conjunctive Mode + the Past Participle of the main verb.

The Conditional Mode can be simple or compound:

Modo Condicional Simples (Simple Conditional Mode). Used to indicate a fact that would happen in the present in the possibility of another fact happening as well.

Example: Se eu pudesse, andaria na bicicleta. (If I could, I would ride the bike.)

Modo Condicional Composto (Compound Conditional Mode). Used to indicate a fact that would've happened in the past in the possibility of another fact having happened as well.

Example: Se eu pudesse, teria andado na bicicleta. (If I could, I would have ridden the bike.)

The Imperative Mode: Anda na bicicleta! (Ride the bike!)

And finally, we have the three nominal forms:

The Infinitive: Eu gosto de andar na bicicleta. (I like to ride the bike.)

The Past Participle: Eu gostava de ter andado na bicicleta. (I would like to have ridden the bike.)

The Gerund: Eu estava sempre andando na bicicleta. (I was always riding the bike.)

6.3 Conjugation of regular verbs

Let's conjugate the verb "Falar" ("To speak"), which is part of the **1st conjugation** group.

INDICATIVE MODE

Present

Eu falo – I speak

Tu falas – You speak

Ele fala – He/she/it speaks

Nós falamos – We speak

Vós falais – You speak

Eles fal<u>am</u> – They speak

Simple Perfect Past

Eu fal<u>ei</u> – I spoke

Tu fal<u>aste</u> – You spoke

Ele fal<u>ou</u> – He/she/it spoke

Nós fal<u>ámos</u> (BR: fal<u>amos</u>) – We spoke

Vós fal<u>astes</u> – You spoke

Eles fal<u>aram</u> – They spoke

Compound Perfect Past

Eu tenho falado – I have spoken

Tu tens falado – You have spoken

Ele tem falado – He/she/it has spoken

Nós temos falado – We have spoken

Vós tendes falado – You have spoken

Eles têm falado – They have spoken

Imperfect Past

Eu fal<u>ava</u> – I used to speak

Tu fal<u>avas</u> – You used to speak

Ele fal<u>ava</u> – He/she/it used to speak

Nós fal<u>ávamos</u> – We used to speak

Vós fal<u>áveis</u> – You used to speak

Eles fal<u>avam</u> – They used to speak

Simple More-than-perfect Past

Eu fal<u>ara</u> – I had spoken

Tu fal<u>aras</u> – You had spoken

Ele fal<u>ara</u> – He/she/it had spoken

Nós fal<u>áramos</u> – We had spoken

Vós fal<u>áreis</u> – You had spoken

Eles fal<u>aram</u> – They had spoken

Compound More-than-perfect Past

Eu tinha falado – I had spoken

Tu tinhas falado – You had spoken

Ele tinha falado – He/she/it had spoken

Nós tínhamos falado – We had spoken

Vós tínheis falado – You had spoken

Eles tinham falado – They had spoken

Simple Future

Eu fal<u>arei</u> – I will speak

Tu fal<u>arás</u> – You will speak

Ele fal<u>ará</u> – He/she/it will speak

Nós fal<u>aremos</u> – We will speak

Vós fal<u>areis</u> – You will speak

Eles fal<u>arão</u> – They will speak

Compound Future

Eu terei falado – I will have spoken

Tu terás falado – You will have spoken

Ele terá falado – He/she/it will have spoken

Nós teremos falado – We will have spoken

Vós tereis falado – You will have spoken

Eles terão falado – They will have spoken

CONJUCTIVE MODE

Present

 (Que) eu fale – (That) I speak

(Que) tu fales – (That) you speak

(Que) ele fale – (That) he/she/it speaks

(Que) nós falemos – (That) we speak

(Que) vós faleis – (That) you speak

(Que) eles falem – (That) they speak

Imperfect Past

(Se) eu falasse – (If) I spoke

(Se) tu falasses – (If) you spoke

(Se) ele falasse – (If) he/she/it spoke

(Se) nós falássemos – (If) we spoke

(Se) vós falásseis – (If) you spoke

(Se) eles falassem – (If) they spoke

Compound Perfect Past

(Embora) eu tenha falado – (Although) I have spoken

(Embora) tu tenhas falado – (Although) you have spoken

(Embora) ele tenha falado – (Although) he/she/it has spoken

(Embora) nós tenhamos falado – (Although) we have spoken

(Embora) vós tenhais falado – (Although) you have spoken

(Embora) eles tenham falado – (Although) they have spoken

Compound More-than-perfect Past

(Embora) eu tivesse falado – (Although) I had spoken

(Embora) tu tivesses falado – (Although) you had spoken

(Embora) ele tivesse falado – (Although) he/she/it had spoken

(Embora) nós tivéssemos falado – (Although) we had spoken

(Embora) vós tivésseis falado – (Although) you had spoken

(Embora) eles tivessem falado – (Although) they had spoken

Simple Future

(Quando) eu falar – (When) I speak

(Quando) tu falares – (When) you speak

(Quando) ele falar – (When) he/she/it speaks

(Quando) nós falarmos – (When) we speak

(Quando) vós falardes – (When) you speak

(Quando) eles falarem – (When) they speak

Compound Future

(Quando) eu tiver falado – (When) I have spoken

(Quando) tu tiveres falado – (When) you have spoken

(Quando) ele tiver falado – (When) he/she/it has spoken

(Quando) nós tivermos falado – (When) we have spoken

(Quando) vós tiverdes falado – (When) you have spoken

(Quando) eles tiverem falado – (When) they have spoken

CONDITIONAL MODE

Simple Conditional

Eu falaria – I would speak

Tu falarias – You would speak

Ele falaria – He/she/it would speak

Nós falaríamos – We would speak

Vós falaríeis – You should speak

Eles falariam – They would speak

Compound Conditiona

Eu teria falado – I would have spoken

Tu terias falado – You would have spoken

Ele teria falado – He/she/it would have spoken

Nós teríamos falado – We would have spoken

Vós teríeis falado – You would have spoken

Eles teriam falado – They would have spoken

IMPERATIVE MODE

(Tu) fala – (You) speak

(Ele) fale – (He/she/it) speak

(Nós) falemos – (We) speak

(Vós) falai – (You) speak

(Eles) falem – (They) speak

Gerund

Falando – Speaking

Past Participle

Falado(a) – Spoken

Let's conjugate the verb "Entender" ("To understand") which is part of the **2ⁿᵈ conjugation group**.

INDICATIVE MODE

Present

Eu entendo – I understand

Tu entendes – You understand

Ele entende – He/she/it understands

Nós entendemos – We understand

Vós entendeis – You understand

Eles entendem – They understand

Simple Perfect Past

Eu entendi – I understood

Tu entendeste – You understood

Ele entendeu – He/she/it understood

Nós entendemos – We understood

Vós entendestes – You understood

Eles entenderam – They understood

Compound Perfect Past

Eu tenho entendido – I have understood

Tu tens entendido – You have understood

Ele tem entendido – He/she/it has understood

Nós temos entendido – We have understood

Vós tendes entendido – You have understood

Eles têm entendido – They have understood

Imperfect Past

Eu entendia – I used to understand

Tu entendias – You used to understand

Ele entendia – He/she/it used to understand

Nós entendíamos – We used to understand

Vós entendíeis – You used to understand

Eles entendiam – They used to understand

Simple More-than-perfect Past

Eu entendera – I understood

Tu entenderas – You understood

Ele entendera – He/she/it understood

Nós entendêramos – We understood

Vós entendêreis – You understood

Eles entenderam – They understood

Compound More-than-perfect Past

Eu tinha entendido – I had understood

Tu tinhas entendido – You had understood

Ele tinha entendido – He/she/it had understood

Nós tínhamos entendido – We had understood

Vós tínheis entendido – You understood

Eles tinham entendido – They had understood

Simple Future

Eu entenderei – I will understand

Tu entenderás – You will understand

Ele entenderá – He/she/it will understand

Nós entenderemos – We will understand

Vós entend<u>ereis</u> – You will understand

Eles entend<u>erão</u> – They will understand

Compound Future

Eu terei entendido – I will have understood

Tu terás entendido – You will have understood

Ele terá entendido – He/she/it will have understood

Nós teremos entendido – We will have understood

Vós tereis entendido – You will have understood

Eles terão entendido – They will have understood

CONJUNCTIVE MODE

Present

(Que) eu entend<u>a</u> – (That) I understand

(Que) tu entend<u>as</u> – (That) you understand

(Que) ele entend<u>a</u> – (That) he/she/it understands

(Que) nós entend<u>amos</u> – (That) we understand

(Que) vós entend<u>ais</u> – (That) you understand

(Que) eles entend<u>am</u> – (That) they understand

Imperfect Past

(Se) eu entend<u>esse</u> – (If) I understood

(Se) tu entend<u>esses</u> – (If) you understood

(Se) ele entend<u>esse</u> – (If) he/she/it understood

(Se) nós entend<u>êssemos</u> – (If) we understood

(Se) vós entend<u>êsseis</u> – (If) you understood

(Se) eles entend<u>essem</u> – (If) they understood

Compound Perfect Past

(Embora) eu tenha entendido – (Although) I have understood

(Embora) tu tenhas entendido – (Although) you have understood

(Embora) ele tenha entendido – (Although) he/she/it has understood

(Embora) nós tenhamos entendido – (Although) we have understood

(Embora) vós tenhais entendido – (Although) you have understood

(Embora) eles tenham entendido – (Although) they have understood

Compound More-than-perfect Past

(Embora) eu tivesse entendido – (Although) I had understood

(Embora) tu tivesses entendido – (Although) you had understood

(Embora) ele tivesse entendido – (Although) he/she/it had understood

(Embora) nós tivéssemos entendido – (Although) we had understood

(Embora) vós tivésseis entendido – (Although) you had understood

(Embora) eles tivessem entendido – (Although) they had understood

Simple Future

(Quando) eu entend<u>er</u> – (When) I understand

(Quando) tu entend<u>eres</u> – (When) you understand

(Quando) ele entend<u>ers</u> – (When) he/she/it understands

(Quando) nós entend<u>ermos</u> – (When) we understand

(Quando) vós entend<u>erdes</u> – (When) you understand

(Quando) eles entend<u>erem</u> – (When) they understand

Compound Future

(Quando) eu tiver entendido – (When) I have understood

(Quando) tu tiveres – (When) you have understood

(Quando) ele tiver – (When) he/she/it has understood

(Quando) nós tivermos – (When) we have understood

(Quando) vós tiverdes – (When) you have understood

(Quando) eles tiverem – (When) they have understood

CONDITIONAL MODE

Simple Conditional

Eu entend<u>eria</u> – I would understand

Tu entend<u>erias</u> – You would understand

Ele entend<u>eria</u> – He/she/it would understand

Nós entend<u>eríamos</u> – We would understand

Vós entend<u>eríeis</u> -You would understand

Eles entend<u>eriam</u> – They would understand

Compound Conditional

Eu teria entendido – I would have understood

Tu terias entendido – You would have understood

Ele teria entendido – He/she/it would have understood

Nós teríamos entendido – We would have understood

Vós teríeis entendido – You would have understood

Eles teriam entendido – They would have understood

IMPERATIVE MODE

(Tu) entend<u>e</u> – (You) understand

(Ele) entend<u>a</u> – (He/she/it) understand

(Nós) entend<u>amos</u> – (We) understand

(Vós) entend<u>ei</u> – (You) understand

(Eles) entend<u>am</u> – (They) understand

Gerund

Entend<u>endo</u> – Understanding

Past Participle

Entend<u>ido(a)</u> – Understood

Let's conjugate the verb "Abrir" ("To open") which is part of the **3rd conjugation group**.

INDICATIVE MODE

Present

Eu abr<u>o</u> – I open

Tu abr<u>es</u> – You open

Ele abr<u>e</u> – He/she/it opens

Nós abr<u>imos</u> – We open

Vós abr<u>is</u> – You open

Eles abr<u>em</u> – They open

Simple Perfect Past

Eu abr<u>i</u> – I opened

Tu abr<u>iste</u> – You opened

Ele abr<u>iu</u> – He/she/it opened

Nós abr<u>imos</u> – We opened

Vós abr<u>istes</u> – You opened

Eles abr<u>iram</u> – They opened

Compound Perfect Past

Eu tenho aberto – I have opened

Tu tens aberto – You have opened

Ele tem aberto – He/she/it has opened

Nós temos aberto – We have opened

Vós tendes aberto – You have opened

Eles têm aberto – They have opened

Imperfect Past

Eu abr<u>ia</u> – I used to open

Tu abr<u>ias</u> – You used to open

Ele abr<u>ia</u> – He/she/it used to open

Nós abr<u>íamos</u> – We used to open

Vós abr<u>íeis</u> – You used to open

Eles abr<u>iam</u> – They used to open

Simple More-than-perfect Past

Eu abr<u>ira</u> – I had opened

Tu abr<u>iras</u> – You had opened

Ele abr<u>ira</u> – He/she/it had opened

Nós abr<u>íramos</u> – We had opened

Vós abr<u>íreis</u> – You had opened

Eles abr<u>iram</u> – They had opened

Compound More-than-perfect Past

Eu tinha aberto – I had opened

Tu tinhas aberto – You had opened

Ele tinha aberto – He/she/it had opened

Nós tínhamos aberto – We had opened

Vós tínheis aberto – You had opened

Eles tinham aberto – They had opened

Simple Future

Eu abrirei – I will open

Tu abrirás – You will open

Ele abrirá – He/she/it will open

Nós abriremos – We will open

Vós abrireis – You will open

Eles abrirão – They will open

Compound Future

Eu terei aberto – I will have opened

Tu terás aberto – You will have opened

Ele terá aberto – He/she/it will have opened

Nós teremos aberto – We will have opened

Vós tereis aberto – You will have opened

Eles terão aberto – They will have opened

CONJUNCTIVE MODE

Present

 (Que) eu abra – (That) I open

(Que) tu abras – (That) you open

(Que) ele abra – (That) he/she/it opens

(Que) nós abramos – (That) we open

(Que) vós abrais – (That) you open

(Que) eles abram – (That) they open

Imperfect Past

(Se) eu abr<u>isse</u> – (If) I opened

(Se) tu abr<u>isses</u> – (If) you opened

(Se) ele abr<u>isse</u> – (If) he/she/it opened

(Se) nós abr<u>íssemos</u> – (If) we opened

(Se) vós abr<u>ísseis</u> – (If) you opened

(Se) eles abr<u>issem</u> – (If) they opened

Compound Perfect Past

(Embora) eu tenha aberto – (Although) I have opened

(Embora) tu tenhas aberto – (Although) you opened

(Embora) ele tenha aberto – (Although) he/she/it opened

(Embora) nós tenhamos aberto – (Although) we opened

(Embora) vós tenhais aberto – (Although) you opened

(Embora) eles tenham aberto – (Although) they opened

Compound More-than-perfect Past

(Embora) eu tivesse aberto – (Although) I have opened

(Embora) tu tivesses aberto – (Although) you opened

(Embora) ele tivesse aberto – (Although) he/she/it opened

(Embora) nós tivéssemos aberto – (Although) we opened

(Embora) vós tivésseis aberto – (Although) you opened

(Embora) eles tivessem aberto – (Although) they opened

Simple Future

(Quando) eu abr<u>ir</u> – (When) I open

(Quando) tu abr<u>ires</u> – (When) you open

(Quando) ele abr<u>ir</u> – (When) he/she/it opens

(Quando) nós abr<u>irmos</u> – (When) we open

(Quando) vós abr<u>irdes</u> – (When) you open

(Quando) eles abr<u>irem</u> – (When) they open

Compound Future

(Quando) eu tiver aberto – (When) I have opened

(Quando) tu tiveres aberto – (When) you have opened

(Quando) ele tiver aberto – (When) he/she/it has opened

(Quando) nós tivermos aberto – (When) we have opened

(Quando) vós tiverdes aberto – (When) you have opened

(Quando) eles tiverem aberto – (When) they have opened

CONDITIONAL MODE

Simple Conditional

Eu abr<u>iria</u> – I would open

Tu abr<u>irias</u> – You would open

Ele abr<u>iria</u> – He/she/it would open

Nós abr<u>iríamos</u> – We would open

Vós abr<u>iríeis</u> – You would open

Eles abr<u>iriam</u> – They would open

Compound Conditional

Eu teria aberto – I would have opened

Tu terias aberto – You would have opened

Ele teria aberto – He/she/it would have opened

Nós teríamos aberto – We would have opened

Vós teríeis aberto – You would have opened

Eles teriam aberto – They would have opened

IMPERAȚIVE MODE

(Tu) abr<u>e</u> – (You) open

(Ele) abr<u>a</u> – (He/she/it) open

(Nós) abr<u>amos</u> – (We) open

(Vós) abr<u>i</u> – (You) open

(Eles) abr<u>am</u> – (They) open

Gerund

Abr<u>indo</u> – Opening

Past Participle

Aberto(a) – Opened

6.4 Conjugation of auxiliary verbs

The verb "Estar" corresponds to the verb "to be" in English, but only in the temporary state of the verb. For example: Ele <u>está</u> bêbado. (He <u>is</u> drunk.); Vocês <u>estão</u> atrasados. (You <u>are</u> late.)

Present

Eu estou – I am

Tu estás – You are

Ele está – He/she/it

Nós estamos – We are

Vós estais – You are

Eles estão – They are

Simple Perfect Past

Eu estive – I was

Tu estiveste – You were

Ele esteve – He/she/it was

Nós estivemos – We were

Vós estivestes – You were

Eles estiveram – They were

Compound Perfect Past

Eu tenho estado – I have been

Tu tens estado – You have been

Ele tem estado – He/she/it has been

Nós temos estado – We have been

Vós tendes estado – You have been

Eles têm estado – They have been

Imperfect Past

Eu estava – I was

Tu estavas – You were

Ele estava – He/she/it was

Nós estávamos – We were

Vós estáveis – You were

Eles estavam – They were

Simple More-than-perfect Past

Eu estivera – I had been

Tu estiveras – You had been

Ele estivera – He/she/it had been

Nós estivéramos – We had been

Vós estivéreis – You had been

Eles estiveram – They had been

Compound More-than-perfect Past

Eu tinha estado – I had been

Tu tinhas estado – You had been

Ele tinha estado – He/she/it had been

Nós tínhamos estado – We had been

Vós tínheis estado – You had been

Eles tinham estado – They had been

Simple Future

Eu estarei – I will be

Tu estarás – You will be

Ele estará – He/she/it will be

Nós estaremos – We will be

Vós estareis – You will be

Eles estarão – They will be

Compound Future

Eu terei estado – I will have been

Tu terás estado – You will have been

Ele terá estado – He/she/it have been

Nós teremos estado – We will have been

Vós tereis estado – You will have been

Eles terão estado – They will have been

CONJUNCTIVE MODE

Present

(Que) eu esteja – (That) I am

(Que) tu estejas – (That) you are

(Que) ele esteja – (That) he/she/it is

(Que) nós estejamos – (That) we are

(Que) vós estejais – (That) you are

(Que) eles estejam – (That) they are

Imperfect Past

(Se) eu estivesse – (If) I was

(Se) tu estivesses – (If) you were

(Se) ele estivesse – (If) he/she/it was

(Se) nós estivéssemos – (If) we were

(Se) vós estivésseis – (If) you were

(Se) eles estivessem – (If) they were

Compound Perfect Past

(Embora) eu tenha estado – (Although) I have been

(Embora) tu tenhas estado – (Although) you have been

(Embora) ele tenha estado – (Although) he/she/it has been

(Embora) nós tenhamos estado – (Although) we have been

(Embora) vós tenhais estado – (Although) you have been

(Embora) eles tenham estado – (Although) they have been

Compound More-than-perfect Past

(Embora) eu tivesse estado – (Although) I had been

(Embora) tu tivesses estado – (Although) you had been

(Embora) ele tivesse estado – (Although) he/she/it had been

(Embora) nós tivéssemos estado – (Although) we had been

(Embora) vós tivésseis estado – (Although) you had been

(Embora) eles tivessem estado – (Although) they had been

Simple Future(Quando) eu estiver – (When) I am

(Quando) tu estiveres – (When) you are

(Quando) ele estiver – (When) he/she/it is

(Quando) nós estivermos – (When) we are

(Quando) vós estiverdes – (When) you are

(Quando) eles estiverem – (When) they are

Compound Future

(Quando) eu tiver estado – (When) I have been

(Quando) tu tiveres estado – (When) you have been

(Quando) ele tiver estado – (When) he/she/it has been

(Quando) nós tivermos estado – (When) we have been

(Quando) vós tiverdes estado – (When) you have been

(Quando) eles tiverem estado – (When) they have been

CONDITIONAL MODE

Simple Conditional

Eu estaria – I would be

Tu estarias – You would be

Ele estaria – He/she/it would be

Nós estaríamos – We would be

Vós estaríeis – You would be

Eles estariam – They would be

Compound Conditional

Eu teria estado – I would have been

Tu terias estado – You would have been

Ele teria estado – He/she/it would have been

Nós teríamos estado – We would have been

Vós teríeis estado – You would have been

Eles teriam estado – They would have been

IMPERATIVE MODE

(Tu) está – (You) be

(Ele) esteja – (He/she/it) be

(Nós) estejamos – (We) be

(Vós) estai – (You) be

(Eles) estejam – (They) be

Gerund

Estando – Being

Past Participle

Estado – Been

The verb "Ter" means "To have".

INDICATIVE MODE

Prsesent

Eu tenho – I have

Tu tens – You have

Ele tem – He/she/it has

Nós temos – We have

Vós tendes – You have

Eles têm – They have

Simple Perfect Past

Eu tive – I had

Tu tiveste – You had

Ele teve – He/she/it had

Nós tivemos – We had

Vós tivestes – You had

Eles tiveram – They had

Compound Perfect Past

Eu tenho tido – I have had

Tu tens tido – You have had

Ele tem tido – He/she/it has had

Nós temos tido – We have had

Vós tendes tido – You have had

Eles têm tido – They have had

Imperfect Past

Eu tinha – I used to have

Tu tinhas – You used to have

Ele tinha – He/she/it used to have

Nós tínhamos – We used to have

Vós tínheis – You used to have

Eles tinham – They used to have

Simple More-than-perfect Past

Eu tivera – I had had

Tu tiveras – You had had

Ele tivera – He/she/it had had

Nós tivéramos – We had had

Vós tivéreis – You had had

Eles tiveram – They had had

More-than-perfect Past

Eu tinha tido – I had had

Tu tinhas tido – You had had

Ele tinha tido – He/she/it had had

Nós tínhamos tido – We had had

Vós tínheis tido – You had had

Eles tinham tido – They had had

Simple Future

Eu terei – I will have

Tu terás – You will have

Ele terá – He/she/it will have

Nós teremos – We will have

Vós tereis – You will have

Eles terão – They will have

Compound Future

Eu terei tido – I will have had

Tu terás tido – You will have had

Ele terá tido – He/she/it will have had

Nós teremos tido – We will have had

Vós tereis tido – You will have had

Eles terão tido – They will have had

CONJUNCTIVE MODE

Present

(Que) eu tenha – (That) I have

(Que) tu tenhas – (That) you have

(Que) ele tenha – (That) he/she/it has

(Que) nós tenhamos – (That) we have

(Que) vós tenhais – (That) you have

(Que) eles tenham – (That) they have

Imperfect Past

(Se) eu tivesse – (If) I had

(Se) tu tivesses – (If) you had

(Se) ele tivesse – (If) he/she/it had

(Se) nós tivéssemos – (If) we had

(Se) vós tivésseis – (If) you had

(Se) eles tivessem – (If) they had

Compound Perfect Past

(Embora) eu tenha tido – (Although) I have had

(Embora) tu tenhas tido – (Although) you have had

(Embora) ele tenha tido – (Although) he/she/it has had

(Embora) nós tenhamos tido – (Although) we have had

(Embora) vós tenhais tido – (Although) you have had

(Embora) eles tenham tido – (Although) they have had

Compound More-than-perfect Past

(Embora) eu tivesse tido – (Although) I had had

(Embora) tu tivesses tido – (Although) you had had

(Embora) ele tivesse tido – (Although) he/she/it had had

(Embora) nós tivéssemos tido – (Although) we had had

(Embora) vós tivésseis tido – (Although) you had had

(Embora) eles tivessem tido – (Although) they had had

Simple Future

(Quando) eu tiver – (When) I have

(Quando) tu tiveres – (When) you have

(Quando) ele tiver – (When) he/she/it has

(Quando) nós tivermos – (When) we have

(Quando) vós tiverdes – (When) you have

(Quando) eles tiverem – (When) they have

Compound Future

(Quando) eu tiver tido – (When) I have had

(Quando) tu tiveres tido – (When) you have had

(Quando) ele tiver tido – (When) he/she/it has had

(Quando) nós tivermos tido – (When) we have had

(Quando) vós tiverdes tido – (When) you have had

(Quando) nós tivermos tido – (When) they have had

CONDITIONAL MODE

Simple Conditional

Eu teria – I would have

Tu terias – You would have

Ele teria – He/she/it would have

Nós teríamos – We would have

Vós teríeis – You would have

Eles teriam – They would have

Compound Conditional

Eu teria tido – I would

Tu terias tido – You would have had

Ele teria tido – He/she/it would have had

Nós teríamos tido – We would have had

Vós teríeis tido – You would have had

Eles teriam tido – They would have had

IMPERATIVE MODE

(Tu) vai – (You) go

(Ele) vá – (He/she/it) go

(Nós) vamos – (We) go

(Vós) ide – (You) go

(Eles) vão – (They) go

Gerund

Indo – Going

Past Participle

Ido – Gone

The verb "Ser" corresponds to the verb "to be" in English, but only in the permanent state of the verb. For example: Eu <u>sou</u> Português. (I <u>am</u> Portuguese.); Nós <u>somos</u> pessoas inteligentes. (We <u>are</u> intelligent people.).

INDICATIVE MODE

Present

Eu sou – I am

Tu és – You are

Ele é – He/she/it is

Nós somos – We are

Vós sois – You are

Eles são – They are

Simple Perfect Past

Eu fui – I was

Tu foste – You were

Ele foi – He/she/it was

Nós fomos – We were

Vós fostes – You were

Eles foram – They were

Compound Perfect Past

Eu tenho sido – I have been

Tu tens sido – You have been

Ele tem sido – He/she/it has been

Nós temos sido – We have been

Vós tendes sido – You have been

Eles têm sido – They have been

Imperfect Past

Eu era – I was

Tu eras – You were

Ele era – He/she/it was

Nós éramos – We were

Vós éreis – You were

Eles eram – They were

Simple More-than-perfect Past

Eu fora – I had been

Tu foras – You had been

Ele fora – He/she/it had been

Nós fôramos – We had been

Vós fôreis – You had been

Eles foram – They had been

Compound More-than-perfect Past

Eu tinha sido – I had been

Tu tinhas sido – You had been

Ele tinha sido – He/she/it had been

Nós tínhamos sido – We had been

Vós tínheis sido – You had been

Eles tinham sido – They had been

Simple Future

Eu serei – I will be

Tu serás – You will be

Ele será – He/she/it will be

Nós seremos – We will be

Vós sereis – You will be

Eles serão – They will be

Compound Future

Eu terei sido – I will have been

Tu terás sido – You will have been

Ele terá sido – He/she/it will have been

Nós teremos sido – We will have been

Vós tereis sido – You will have been

Eles terão sido – They will have been

CONJUNCTIVE MODE

Present

(Que) eu seja – (That) I am

(Que) tu sejas – (That) you are

(Que) ele seja – (That) he/she/it is

(Que) nós sejamos – (That) we are

(Que) vós sejais – (That) you are

(Que) eles sejam – (That) they are

Imperfect Past

(Se) eu fosse – (If) I was

(Se) tu fosses – (If) you were

(Se) ele fosse – (If) he/she/it was

(Se) nós fôssemos – (If) we were

(Se) vós fôsseis – (If) you were

(Se) eles fossem – (If) they were

Compound Perfect Past

(Embora) eu tenha sido – (Although) I have been

(Embora) tu tenhas sido – (Although) you have been

(Embora) ele tenha sido – (Although) he/she/it has been

(Embora) nós tenhamos sido – (Although) we have been

(Embora) vós tenhais sido – (Although) you have been

(Embora) eles tenham sido – (Although) they have been

Compound More-than-perfect Past

(Embora) eu tivesse sido – (Although) I had been

(Embora) tu tivesses sido – (Although) you had been

(Embora) ele tivesse sido – (Although) he/she/it had been

(Embora) nós tivéssemos sido – (Although) we had been

(Embora) vós tivésseis sido – (Although) you had been

(Embora) eles tivessem sido – (Although) they had been

Simple Future

(Quando) eu for – (When) I am

(Quando) tu fores – (When) you are

(Quando) ele for – (When) he/she/it is

(Quando) nós formos – (When) we are

(Quando) vós fordes – (When) you are

(Quando) eles forem – (When) they are

Compound Future

(Quando) eu tiver sido – (When) I have been

(Quando) tu tiveres sido – (When) you have been

(Quando) ele tiver sido – (When) he/she/it has been

(Quando) nós tivermos sido – (When) we have been

(Quando) vós tiverdes sido – (When) you have been

(Quando) eles tiverem sido – (When) they have been

CONDITIONAL MODE

Simple Conditional

Eu seria – I would be

Tu serias – You would be

Ele seria – He/she/it would be

Nós seríamos – We would be

Vós seríeis – You would be

Eles seriam – They would be

Compound Conditional

Eu teria sido – I would have been

Tu terias sido – You would have been

Ele teria sido – He/she/it would have been

Nós teríamos sido – We would have been

Vós teríeis sido – You would have been

Eles teriam sido – They would have been

IMPERATIVE MODE

(Tu) sê – (You) be

(Ele) seja – (He/she/it) be

(Nós) sejamos – (We) be

(Vós) sede – (You) be

(Eles) sejam – (They) be

Gerund

Sendo – Being

Past Participle

Sido – Been

As previously mentioned in *Chapter 3 – Pronouns*, even though the personal pronoun "você" (equivalent to "tu") is considered to be a colloquialism, and for that reason it never shows up in any verb conjugation table, it is used and you must know how to correctly conjugate the verbs for this particular pronoun. So how does that work? Easy. "Você" conjugates the verbs the same way as the personal pronoun "ele" ("he"). It's very important that you pay attention to that aspect. For example:

"You live in Portugal." would be "Você mora em Portugal". (Verb MORAR, regular from the 1st conjugation group).

Likewise, when it comes to "vocês" (equivalent to "vós") you must conjugate the verb the same way as you would for the pronoun "eles". For example:

"You're always welcome." would be "Vocês são sempre bem-vindos." (Verb SER, irregular from the 2nd conjugation group).

Chapter 7 – Conjunctions

Conjunctions, or **conjunções** in Portuguese, are words that connect different sentences. Conjunctions can belong to different categories, depending on the idea they want to convey between the sentences.

7.1 Coordinative conjunctions

The coordinative conjunctions, or **conjunções coordenativas** in Portuguese, connect parts of a sentence that possess a similar meaning. They can be of five different types:

Copulative (copulative) or **additive (aditivas)**, which imply a connection between words or parts of the sentence.

Examples:

A Cláudia e o Rodrigo foram fazer uma caminhada. (Claudia and Rodrigo went for a walk.)

Ela gosta de batatas fritas, mas também de vegetais.

Adversative (adversativas), which indicate an opposition of ideas or a sense of restriction.

Examples:

Fui lá, mas ele não veio. (I went there but he didn't come.)

Receberam o convite, <u>contudo</u> não vieram. (They received the invitation, however they didn't come.)

O Ricardo estava nervoso, <u>porém</u> nada justifica o seu comportamento. (Ricardo was nervous, however nothing justifies his behaviour.)

Disjunctive (disjuntivas) or **alternative (alternativas)**, which express an exclusion or an alternative.

Examples:

Entras <u>ou</u> sais? (Are you coming in or not?)

<u>Ora</u> chega tarde, <u>ora</u> não vem. (He either arrives late or doesn't come at all.)

Vou sair de qualquer maneira, <u>quer</u> chova, <u>quer</u> faça sol. (I'm leaving either way, rain or shine.)

Conclusive (conclusivas), which express a conclusion taken from the previous clause.

Examples:

O carro avariou, <u>portanto</u> temos que o consertar. (The car broke down, consequently we have to fix it.)

O jogo estava viciado, <u>logo</u> não poderia dar certo. (The game was rigged, thus it would never work.)

Explicative (explicativas), which connect the first clause to another one that explains the idea on it. They express a relation of justification, reason or motive.

Examples:

Fecha a porta <u>que</u> está a chover. (Close the door, (since) it's raining.)

See below the most common examples of coordinative conjunctions for each category:

Copulativas / aditivas – E, nem, não só… mas também, não só… como também, bem como, nem, etc.

Adversativas – Mas, porém, todavia, contudo, entretanto, no entanto, etc.

Disjuntivas / alternativas – Ou...ou; ora...ora; quer...quer; já...já, seja... seja, etc.

Conclusivas – Logo, portanto, por isso, assim, por conseguinte, pois, assim, etc.

Explicativas – Que, porque, portanto, pois, etc.

7.2 Subordinative conjunctions

The subordinative conjunctions, or **conjunções subordinativas** in Portuguese, connect prepositions or clauses that depend on each other, since only together they can make sense. They can be of nine different types:

Causal (causais), which express a cause, a reason or a motif.

Examples:

Ele nao veio <u>porque</u> estava doente. (He didn't come because he was sick.)

<u>Como</u> não vimos outro local aberto, viemos para cá. (Since we didn't see another place that was open place, we came here.)

Ele saiu mais cedo <u>uma vez que</u> o filho dele ligou. (He left earlier because his son called.)

Consecutive (consecutivas), which indicate a consequence.

Examples:

Falou <u>tanto</u> na reunião <u>que</u> ficou rouco. (He spoke so much at the meeting, that he became hoarse.)

Ninguém se manifestou, <u>de forma que</u> pensei que todos estavam de acordo. (No one spoke up, therefore I though everyone agreed.)

Comparative (comparativas), which establish a comparison.

Examples:

Tudo correu <u>conforme</u> o previsto. (Everything went according to planned.)

Demorei <u>mais</u> tempo <u>do que</u> gostaria. (I took more time than I would have liked.)

Ela é alta <u>que nem</u> uma girafa. (She's as tall as a giraffe.)

Conformativas, which express the accordance of a certain thought with the main clause.

Example:

As instruções de montagem devem ser seguidas <u>conforme</u> o manual do aparelho. (The assembly instructions should be followed according to the device's manual.)

Concessive (concessivas), which express a reason that is being conceded.

Example:

<u>Embora</u> ficasse nervosa, ela saía-se sempre bem. (Even though she got nervous, she would always do fine.)

Condicional (condicionais), which express a condition necessary for the action to be completed.

Examples:

<u>Se</u> o visse agora, não o reconheceria. (If I saw him now, I wouldn't recognize him.)

<u>Caso</u> eles não cheguem, começamos sem eles. (In case they don't arrive, we start without them.)

Proporcional (proporcionais), which initiate a clause by mentioning a fact that took place or is taking place simultaneously with the one depicted in the main clause.

Example:

À medida que todos foram saindo, a sala começou a esvaziar. (As everyone left, the room started to empty.)

Final (finais), which indicate the purpose that justifies the completion (or not) of certain action.

Examples:

Dei-lhe o comprimido a fim de que aliviasse a dor. (I gave him the pill in order to relieve the pain.)

Convidei-o para que ele não ficasse chateado. (I invited him so that he wouldn't be upset.)

Comecei os preparativos cedo de modo a que tudo ficasse pronto a horas. (I started the preparations early, so that everything was ready on time.)

Temporal (temporais), which express circumstances that relate to time.

Examples:

Quando cheguei ela já não estava. (When I arrived, she wasn't there anymore.)

Assim que a Sara chegar, avisa-me. (Let me know as soon as Sara arrives.)

See below the most common conjunctions in each category:

Causais – Porque, uma vez que, sendo que, visto que, como, etc.

Consecutivas – Que (preceeded by tal, tão, tanto, tamanho), sem que, de modo que, de forma que, etc.

Comparativas – Como, tal qual, que ou do que, assim como, bem como, que nem, tão…como, mais…que, menos…que, tanto…como, etc.

Conformativas – Conforme, segundo, consoante, etc.

Concessivas – Mesmo que, por mais que, ainda que, se bem que, embora, etc.

Condicionais – Se, caso, contanto que, a menos que, sem que, salvo se, excepto se, na condição de, a não ser que, desde que, no caso que, etc.

Proporcionais – À medida que, à proporção que, quanto mais, quanto menos, etc.

Finais – A fim de que, para que, etc.

Temporais – Quando, enquanto, mal, apenas, antes que, assim que, desde que, cada vez que, até que, todas as vezes que, sempre que, logo que, depois que, etc.

Chapter 8 – Useful expressions and vocabulary

You can find below some of the most common expressions that will certainly be very useful if you want to get around in a Portuguese speaking country. Every time you see 'PT' it means that is a vocabulary and /or expression used in Portugal; when you see 'BR' that means the vocabulary and / or expression presented is used in Brazil.

8.1 Meeting and greeting people

Olá – Hello

Oi – Hi

Bom dia – Good morning

Boa tarde – Good afternoon

Boa noite – Good evening

PT: Bom fim-de-semana – Have a nice weekend

BR: Bom final-de-semana – Have a nice weekend

Tchau – Bye

Até logo – See you later

Até já – See you soon

Adeus – Goodbye

Até amanhã – See you tomorrow

PT: Como te chamas? [1] – What's your name?

PT: Como se chama? [2] – What's your name?

BR: Qual o seu nome? – What's your name?

PT: Chamo-me ___ [3] – My name is ___.

BR: O meu nome é ___ [3] – My name is ___.

PT: Quantos anos tens? – How old are you?

PT: Quantos anos você tem? – How old are you?

BR: Qual a sua idade? – How old are you?

Tenho ___ anos – I'm ___ years old

PT: Onde é que moras? [1] – Where do you live?

PT: Onde é que mora? [2] – Where do you live?

BR: Onde você mora? – Where do you live?

Moro em ___. – I live in ___.

PT: Falas inglês? [1] – Do you speak English?

PT/BR: Você fala inglês? [2] – Do you speak English?

PT: Onde fica a casa-de-banho? – Where's the bathroom?

BR: Onde fica o banheiro? – Where's the bathroom?

Sim – Yes

Não – No

Obrigado – Thank you / Thanks

Obrigada – Thank you / Thanks

PT: Desculpa [1] – Sorry

PT/BR: Desculpe [2] – Sorry

Por favor – Please

PT: Se faz favor – Please

Parabéns! – Congratulations!

[1] This is used in an informal European Portuguese speech.

[2] This is used in a formal European Portuguese speech.

[3] When answering this question in real life situations, is always more natural to just say your name (e.g. Answer 'Débora' instead of saying 'Chamo-me Débora'.)

A person's first name is called simply their "nome" ("name"). Their last name or group of last names are called "apelidos" in European Portuguese and "sobrenomes" in Brazilian Portuguese.

8.2 Interjections

Interjection, or **interjeições** in Portuguese, are words that express a spontaneous feeling or reaction.

Ah! – Ah!

Ai! – Ouch!

Bravo! – Bravo!

Calma! – Take it easy!

Chega! – Enough!

Ei! – Hey!

Força! – Go ahead!

Meu Deus! – My God!

Nossa! – Oh my!

Oh! – Aww!

Que pena! – What a pity!

Que susto! – What a scare!

Porra! – Damn!

Psiu! – Pssst!

PT: Santinho! – God bless you!

BR: Saúde! – God bless you!

Uau! – Wow!

Viva! – Hooray!

8.3 Cardinal numbers

Some cardinal numbers vary in gender. The numbers 1 and 2, for instance, admit both masculine and feminine forms, depending if the object they're referring to is masculine or feminine. 1 can be either "um" or "uma", and 2 can be either "dois" or "duas". This rule also applies to their derivations: 21 can be either "vinte e um" or "vinte e uma". When we're in the hundreds category, every "centena" can also be either masculine or feminine (e.g. 500 can be either "quinhentos" or "quinhentas"). Check the pronunciation on the last column.

0 – Zero [z(m)eh-roo]

1 – Um / uma [oom / oomuh]

2 – Dois / duas [dôys / doo-us]

3 – Três [tra(y)s]

4 – Quatro [kooah-troo]

5 – Cinco [sin-koo]

6 – Seis [saysh]

7 – Sete [s(m)eh-tuh]

8 – Oito [oy-too]

9 – Nove [naw-vuh]

10 – Dez [dash]

11 – Onze [ôn-zuh]

12 – Doze [dô-zuh]

13 – Treze [tra(y)-zuh]

14 – Catorze [kah-tôr-zuh]

15 – Quinze [keen-zuh]

16 – PT: Dezasseis / BR: Dezesseis [duh-zah-saysh] / [duh-zeh-saysh]

17 – PT: Dezassete / BR: Dezessete [duh-zuh-s(m)eh-tuh] / [duz-zeh-s(m)eh-tee]

18 – Dezoito [duh-zôy-too]

19 – PT: Dezanove / BR: Dezenove [duh-zuh-naw-vuh] / [da(y)-za(y)-naw-vee]

20 – Vinte [vin-tuh]

21 – Vinte e um / vinte e uma [vin-tuh-ee-oom / oomuh]

23 – Vinte e três [vin-tuh-ee-tra(y)s]

30 – Trinta [treen-tuh]

40 – Quarenta [kua-ren-tuh]

50 – Cinquenta [sin-kuen-tuh]

60 – Sessenta [suh-sem-tuh]

70 – Setenta [suh-tent-tuh]

80 – Oitenta [oy-tem-tuh]

90 – Noventa [noo-vem-tuh]

100 – Cem [saym]

101 – Cento e um / cento e uma [sem-too-ee-oom / oomuh]

102 – Cento e dois / cento e duas [sem-too-ee-dôys /doo-us]

200 – Duzentos / duzentas [doo-zen-toos / -tuhs]

300 – Trezentos / trezentas [tru-zen-toos/-tuhs]

400 – Quatrocentos / quatrocentas [kua-troo-sem-toos/ -tuhs]

500 – Quinhentos / quinhentas [kee-ñen-toos / -tuhs]

600 – Seiscentos / seiscentas [says-sem-toos / -tuhs]

700 – Setecentos / setecentas [s(m)eh-tuh-sem-toos/-tuhs]

800 – Oitocentos / oitocentas [oy-too-sem-toos / -tuhs]

900 – Novecentos / novecentas [naw-vuh-sem-toos / -tuhs]

1.000 – Mil [mill]

2.000 – Dois mil / duas mil [dôys-mil / doo-us-mill]

10.000 – Dez mil [dash-mill]

300.000 – Trezentos mil / trezentas mil [truh-zen-toos-mill / -tuhs-mill]

1.000.000 – Um milhão [oom-millâum]

1.500.000 – Um milhão e quinhentos mil / um milhão e quinhentas mil [oom-millâum-ee-kee-ñen-toos-mill / -tuhs-mil]

8.4 Ordinal numbers

Just like the cardinal numbers, ordinal numbers may also vary in number and gender. This means that in every ordinal number you're about to see (they're presented in the masculine form), to switch them to the feminine form all you have to do is drop the O and place an A at the end, and in the abbreviated form the feminine form is 1ª instead of 1º. From 11º onwards, you just have to combine the names of the individual ordinal elements. For example, 125º would be centésimo (100º) vigésimo (20º) terceiro (3º), so you just have to apply the ordinal denomination for each numeric unit.

1º - Primeiro [pree-may-roo]

2º - Segundo [suh-goon-doo]

3º - Terceiro [tuhr-say-roo]

4º - Quarto [kooar-too]

5º - Quinto [keen-too]

6º - Sexto [saysh-too]

7º - Sétimo [s(m)eh-tee-moo]

8º - Oitavo [oy-tah-voo]

9º - Nono [nô-noo]

10º - Décimo [d(m)eh-see-moo]

11º - Décimo-primeiro [d(m)eh-see-moo-pree-may-roo]

12º - Décimo-segundo [d(m)eh-see-moo-suh-goon-doo]

20º - Vigésimo [vee-g(m)eh-zee-moo]

30º - Trigésimo [tree-g(m)eh-zee-moo]

40º - Quadrigésimo [kuah-druh-g(m)eh-zee-moo]

50º - Quinquagésimo [keen-kua-g(m)eh-zee-moo]

60º - Sexagésimo [s(m)eh-ksuh-g(m)eh-zee-moo]

70º - Septuagésimo [cep-too-uh-g(m)eh-zee-moo]

80º - Octogésimo [octoo-uh-g(m)eh-zee-moo]

90º - Nonagésimo [nô-nuh-g(m)eh-zee-moo]

100º - Centésimo [sen-t(m)eh-zee-moo]

101º - Centésimo-primeiro [sem-t(m)eh-zee-moo-pree-may-roo]

200º - Ducentésimo [doo-sem-t(m)eh-zee-moo]

300º - Trecentésimo [truh-sem-t(m)eh-zee-moo]

400° - Quadringentésimo [kua-dreen-gen-t(m)eh-zee-moo]

500° - Quingentésimo [keen-gen-t(m)eh-zee-moo]

600° - Seiscentésimo [saysh-sem-t(m)eh-zee-moo]

700° - Septingentésimo [cep-teen-gen-t(m)eh-zee-moo]

800° - Octingentésimo [oc-teen-gen-t(m)eh-zee-moo]

900° - Nongentésimo [non-gen-t(m)eh-zee-moo]

1000° - Milésimo [mee-l(m)eh-zee-moo]

8.5 Telling the time

In general, the period from 0h to 12:59h is considered "manhã" ("morning").

The period from 13h to 19:59h is considered "tarde" ("afternoon").

The period from 20h to 23:59h is considered "noite" (evening).

It's important to mention that the time is normally written in 24 hours format, especially in European Portuguese. However, people normally say it in 12-hour format. So, how does that work? Simple, to differentiate 6h from 18h (6 AM from 6 PM), people say "seis da manhã" ("six in the morning") and "seis da tarde" ("six in the afternoon"). Another example:

8h vs 20h (8 AM vs 8 PM) – oito da manhã (eight in the morning) vs oito da noite (eight in the evening).

To say the time, you should always use the verb "ser" in the plural form. For example:

4:00 / 16:00 – São quatro horas (It's four o'clock)

2:00 / 14:00 – São duas horas (It's two o'clock)

These cases are an exception:

1:00 / 13:00 – É uma hora (It's one o'clock)

12:00 – É meio-dia (It's noon)

0:00 – É meia-noite (It's midnight)

Note that you don't necessarily need to say it's four <u>in the morning</u> or four <u>in the afternoon</u>. You can say that but people commonly just say "It's ___ hours".

If you want to mention half-hours, you should add "e meia" (and a half) or "e trinta" (and thirty). The first one is much more common. For example:

4:30 – São quatro e meia / São quatro e trinta (literally "It's four and a half" / "It's four thirty")

If you want to mention 15 minutes, you should say "e um quarto" (and a quarter) or "e quinze" (and fifteen), since 15 minutes represent a quarter of an hour (60 minutes). The first one only applies to European Portuguese. For example:

18:15 – São seis e um quarto / São seis e quinze (literally "It's six and a quarter" / "It's six fifteen")

Another way you can say the time is by stating how many minutes are left to turn the hour. For example:

3:45 – São quinze para as quatro (literally "It's fifteen until four")

In European Portuguese would also be common to say in this situation "São quatro menos um quarto." (literally "It's four minus a quarter.").

8.6 Dates

The days of the week are as follow. After the dash you can see the short form of saying each day, which are more commonly used.

Segunda-feira / Segunda – Monday

Terça-feira / Terça – Tuesday

Quarta-feira / Quarta – Wednesday

Quinta-feira / Quinta – Thursday

Sexta-feira / Sexta – Friday

Sábado – Saturday

Domingo – Sunday

The calendar months are as follow:

Janeiro – January

Fevereiro – February

Março – March

Abril – April

Maio – May

Junho – June

Julho – July

Agosto – August

Setembro – September

Outubro – October

Novembro – November

Dezembro – December

To mention a specific year you should simply read the full number. Different from English, you should not associate pairs of numbers when you read them. Just read the whole number, even if it seems longer that way.

Examples:

1995 – Mil novecentos e noventa e cinco (One thousand nine hundred and ninety-five)

2000 – Dois mil (Two thousand)

2015 – Dois mil e quinze (Two thousand and fifteen)

2030 – Dois mil e trinta (Two thousand and thirty)

A full date should be written as follows:

Domingo, 10 de junho de 2018

Note that you should always use "de" between the day and the month and again between the month and the year. This is because that specific day belongs to the month of June, which belongs to the year of 2018.

In abbreviated form:

10/18/2018 (MM/DD/YYYY), always from the most specific time period (day) to the broadest time period (year).

Check the seasons of the year below:

Primavera – Spring

Verão – Summer

Outono – Fall

Inverno – Winter

And the main festive days:

Ano Novo – New Year's

Carnaval – Carnival

Páscoa – Easter

Natal – Christmas

Aniversário – Birthday

8.7 Family

Pai [pie] – Father

Mãe [mâe] – Mother

Filho [fee-llioo] – Son

Filha [fee-lliuh] – Daughter

Irmão [eer-mâu] – Brother

Irmã [eer-muh] – Sister

Tio [tee-oo] – Uncle

Tia [tee-uh] – Aunt

Sobrinho [soo-bree-ñoo] – Nephew

Sobrinha [soo-bree-ñuh] – Niece

Primo [pree-moo] – Cousin

Prima [pree-muh] – Cousin

Avô [uh-vô] – Grandfather

Avó [uh-vaw] – Grandmother

Neto [n(m)eh-too] – Grandson

Neta [n(m)eh-tuh] – Granddaughter

Bisavô [bee-zuh-vô] – Greatgrandfather

Bisavó [bee-zuh-vaw] – Greatgrandmother

Padrinho [puh-dree-ño] – Godfather

Madrinha [muh-dree-ña] – Godmother

Enteado [en-tee-ah-doo] – Step-son

Enteada [en-tee-ah-duh] – Step-daughter

Cunhado [coo-ña-doo] – Brother-in-law

Cunhada [coo-ña-duh] – Sister-in-law

Sogro [sô-groo] – Father-in-law

Sogra [saw-gruh] – Mother-in-law

8.8 Colors

Amarelo – Yellow

Azul – Blue

Azul claro – Light blue

Branco – White

Castanho / <u>BR</u>: Marrom – Brown

Cinzento / <u>BR</u>: Cinza – Grey

Dourado – Golden

Laranja – Orange

Preto – Black

Prateado – Silver

Rosa – Pink

Roxo – Purple

Verde – Green

Verde claro – Light green

Vermelho – Red

8.9 Animals

Cão – Dog

Gato – Cat

Formiga – Ant

Morcego – Bat

Urso – Bear

Abelha – Bee

Touro – Bull

Borboleta – Butterfly

Camelo – Camel

Vaca – Cow

Crocodilo – Crocodile

Pato – Duck

Elefante – Elephant

Peixe – Fish

Sapo – Frog

Girafa – Giraffe

Galinha – Hen

Cavalo – Horse

Leão – Lion

Lagosta – Lobster

Macaco – Monkey

Rato – Mouse

Papagaio – Parrot

Pombo – Pidgeon

Porco – Pig

Coelho – Rabbit

Foca – Seal

Ovelha – Sheep

Caracol – Snail

Cobra – Snake

Tigre – Tiger

Atum – Tuna

Tartaruga – Turtle

Baleia – Whale

Lobo – Wolf

Zebra – Zebra

8.10 Countries and nationalities

When it comes to countries, the majority of them is considered to be feminine; some are masculine and very few are gender neutral. On the table below you will see the gender attributed to each country. The article "a" is used before countries considered to be feminine and "o" is used for masculine countries. Every time you see (-) before the name of the country in the next table, that means it is gender neutral.

(-) Portugal (Portugal); Português / Portuguesa

(o) Brasil (Brazil); Brasileiro / Brasileira

(a) Áustria (Austria); Austríaco / Austríaca

(a) Bélgica (Belgium); Belga

(o) Canadá (Canada); Canadiano / Canadiana (BR: Canadense)

(a) China (China); Chinês / Chinesa

(a) Croácia (Croatia); Croata

(a) Dinamarca (Denmark); Dinamarquês / Dinamarquesa

(a) Inglaterra (England); Inglês / Inglesa

(a) Finlândia (Finland); Finlandês / Finlandesa

(a) França (France); Francês / Francesa

(a) Alemanha (Germany); Alemão / Alemã

(a) Grécia (Greece); Grego / Grega

(a) Hungria (Hungary); Húngaro / Húngara

(a) Índia (India); Indiano / Indiana

(a) Irlanda (Ireland); Irlandês / Irlandesa

(a) Itália (Italy); Italiano / Italiana

(o) Japão (Japan); Japonês / Japonesa

(a) Coreia (Korea); Coreano / Coreana

(-) Luxemburgo (Luxembourg); Luxemburguês / Luxemburguesa

(o) México (Mexico); Mexicano / Mexicana

(a) Holanda (Netherlands); Holandês / Holandesa

(a) Polónia (BR: Polônia) (Poland); Polaco (BR: Polonês) / Polaca (BR: Polonesa)

(a) Roménia (BR: Romênia) (Romania); Romeno / Romena

(a) Rússia (Russia); Russo / Russa

(a) Espanha (Spain); Espanhol / Espanhola

(a) Suécia (Sweden); Sueco / Sueca

(a) Suíça (Switzerland); Suíço / suíça

(a) Turquia (Turkey); Turco / Turca

(os) Estados Unidos (United States); Estadunidense (Americano)

8.11 Professions / Jobs

Accountant – Contabilista

Actor / Actress – Ator / Atriz

Architect – Arquiteto(a)

Attorney – Procurador(a)

Baker – Padeiro(a)

Barber – Barbeiro(a)

Butcher – Talhante / BR: Açougueiro(a)

Carpenter – Carpinteiro(a)

Cashier – Caixa

Dentist – Dentista

Doctor – Médico(a)

Engineer – Engenheiro(a)

Farmer – Agricultor / Agricultora

Gardener – Jardineiro(a)

Hair dresser – Cabeleiro(a)

Journalist – Jornalista

Judge – Juiz / Juíza

Lawyer – Advogado(a)

Manager – Gerente

Nurse – Enfermeiro(a)

Pharmacist – Farmacêutico(a)

Postman – Carteiro(a)

Priest – Padre

Surgeon – Cirurgião / Cirurgiã

Teacher; Professor – Professor / Professora

Waiter / Waitress – Empregado(a) de mesa / BR: Garçon / Garçonete

8.12 Getting around

Over the next sub-sections you'll find vocabulary and common phrases that will be very useful in specific situations or environments.

8.12.1 At the airport

Airplane – Avião

Airport – Aeroporto

Airport terminal – Terminal do Aeroporto

Boarding gate – Portão de embarque

Customs – Alfândega

Control tower – Torre de controlo / BR: Torre de controle

Economy class – Classe económica / BR: Classe econômica

First class – Primeira classe

Flight – Voo

Landing runway – Pista de aterragem / BR: Pista de aterrissagem

Luggage – Bagagem; Malas

On board – A bordo

Passengers – Passageiros

Passport(s) – Passaporte(s)

Pilot – Piloto(a)

Turbine - Turbina

Wings – Asas

Seat – Assento

Stewardess – Hospedeira / BR: Aeromoça

Take off – Descolagem / BR: Decolagem

Ticket – Passagem; bilhete

Trip – Viagem

Could you tell me what time is the next flight to Paris, please? – Pode dizer-me (BR: me dizer) a que horas sai o próximo voo para Paris, por favor?

Does this plane go straight to Paris? – O avião vai diretamente para Paris?

How much luggage can I take? – Quanta bagagem posso levar?

I want to check this luggage. – Quero despachar estas malas.

I would like a window seat. – Gostaria de um lugar próximo à janela.

This is my first flight. – É a primeira vez que ando de avião.

My seatbelt is not working. – O meu cinto de segurança não está a funcionar. (BR: O meu cinto de segurança não está funcionando.)

Do you serve meals during the flight? – Servem refeições durante o voo?

Could you bring me some water, please? – Pode trazer-me (BR: me trazer) uma água, por favor?

How much time left for the landing? – Quanto tempo falta para a aterragem? / BR: Quanto tempo falta para a aterrissagem?

Is there any bus / shuttle leaving the airport for the downtown? – Há algum autocarro (BR: ônibus) do aeroporto para o centro da cidade?

8.12.2 In the city

Bank – Banco

Building – Edifício

Bus – Autocarro / BR: Ônibus

Church – Igreja

City – Cidade

Closed – Fechado(a)

Factory – Fábrica

Gas station – Bomba de gasoline / BR: Posto de gasoline

Library – Biblioteca

Mall – Shopping

Monument – Monumento

Museum – Museu

Neighborhood – Bairro

Open – Aberto(a)

Park – Parque

Pedestrian – Peão / BR: Pedestre

Skyscrapercity – Arranha-céus

Square – Praça

Stadium – Estádio

Statue – Estátua

Store – Loja

Street – Rua

Subway – Metro / BR: Metrô

Town hall – Câmara Municipal / BR: Prefeitura

Traffic – Engarrafamento; Trânsito

Traffic light – Semáforo / BR: Sinal de trânsito

Ask for directions. – Pergunta o caminho.

How do I get to the main square? – Como chego até à praça principal?

Is that far from here? – Isso fica longe daqui?

Is only a few steps away. – Fica a alguns passos de distância.

Turn left. – Vire à esquerda.

Turn right. – Vire à direita.

Go straight forward. – Siga em frente.

Go up the street. – Suba a rua.

Go down the street. – Desça a rua.

What's that? – O que é aquilo?

What are the opening hours of the museum? – Qual o horário de funcionamento do museu?

What street is this? – Como se chama esta rua? / BR: Qual o nome dessa rua?

8.12.3 At the hotel

Bed – Cama

(Double) bed – Cama de casal

(Single) bed – Cama de solteiro

Bill – Conta

Breakfast – Pequeno-almoço / BR: Café da manhã

Corridor – Corredor

Credit card – Cartão de crédito

Doorman – Porteiro

Floor – Andar

Guest – Hóspede

Hall – Hall

Hot water – Água quente

Hotel – Hotel

Lift / Elevator – Elevador

Lounge – Salão

Key(s) – Chave(s)

Recepcionist – Recepcionista

Registration – Registo

Room – Quarto

(Single) room – Quarto de solteiro

Room number 103 – Quarto número 103

Room service – Serviço de quarto

Stairs – Escadas

Waiter – Empregado de mesa / BR: Garçon

Wake-up service – Serviço despertar; Serviço despertador

Does the price include breakfast? – O preço inclui pequeno-almoço? / BR: O preço inclui café da manhã?

What's the room number? – Qual é o número do quarto?

This room is too small. – Este quarto é pequeno demais.

This room is too big. – Este quarto é grande demais.

I want a room with a double bed. – Quero um quarto com cama de casal.

I want a room with a nice view to the city. – Quero um quarto com uma boa vista para a cidade.

8.12.4 At the bank

ATM Machine – Caixa Multibanco / BR: Caixa eletrônico

Bank – Banco

Branch – Filial

(To) cash a check – Depositar um cheque

Counter – Balcão

Credit – Crédito

Debit – Débito

(To) deposit money – Depositar dinheiro

Exchange rate – Taxa de câmbio

Bondsman – Fiador

Insurance – Seguro

Interest rates – Taxas de juro

Investment – Investimento

Mortgage – Hipoteca

Opening a bank account – Abrir uma conta

(To) print a bank account – Tirar o saldo da conta / BR: Tirar o extrato da conta

Stock market – Bolsa de valores

Stocks – Ações

(To) transfer money – Transferir dinheiro

(To) withdraw money – Levantar dinheiro / BR: Sacar dinheiro

I want to deposit this money. – Quero depositar este dinheiro.

Where is the nearest branch of this bank? – Onde fica a filial mais próxima deste banco?

I want to raise a loan. – Quero contrair um empréstimo.

I have a bondsman. – Eu tenho um fiador.

8.12.5 Shopping

The currency used in Portugal is the Euro, which is divided into cents coins, euro coins and euro notes. Cêntimo is pronounced [sen-tee-moo] (Cêntimos [sen-tee-moosh]) and Euro is pronounced [êu-roo] (Euros [êu-roosh]).

Euro coins:

Um (1) cêntimo

Dois (2) cêntimos

Cinco (5) cêntimos

Dez (10) cêntimos

Vinte (20) cêntimos

Cinquenta (50) cêntimos

Um (1) euro

Dois (2) euros

Euro bank notes:

Cinco (5) euros

Dez (10) euros

Vinte (20) euros

Cinquenta (50) euros

Cem (100) euros

Duzentos (200) euros

Quinhentos (500) euros

The currency used in Brazil is the Real, which is divided into cents coins, real coins and real bank notes. Centavo is pronounced [sen-tah-voo] (Centavos [sen-tah-voosh]) and Real is pronounced [rê-ow] (Reais [rê-eish]).

Real coins are as follow:

Um (1) centavo

Cinco (5) centavos

Dez (10) centavos

Vinte e cinco (25) centavos

Cinquenta (50) centavos

Um (1) real

Real bank notes are as follow:

Dois (2) reais

Cinco (5) reais

Dez (10) reais

Vinte (20) reais

Cinquenta (50) reais

Cem (100) reais

General vocabulary and phrases

Cash sale – Pronto pagamento

Change – Troco

Cheap – Barato(a)

Credit – Crédito

Debit – Débito

Discount – Desconto

Expensive – Caro(a)

Fitting room – Provador

Installment payment – Pagamento em prestações

On sale – Em promoção

Size – Tamanho

(To) try on – Experimentar

How much? – Quanto custa?

Do you have a different size? – Tem outro tamanho?

Can you make a discount? – Pode fazer um desconto?

Is it possible to buy on installments? – É possível pagar em prestações?

I want to buy a pair of shoes. – Quero comprar um par de sapatos.

8.12.6 At the restaurant

Fruits and vegetables

Apple – Maçã

Apricot – Alperce

Banana – Banana

Cabbage – Couve

Carrot – Cenoura

Cherry / Cherries – Cereja(s)

Coconut – Coco

Grape(s) – Uva(s)

Lemon – Limão

Lettuce – Alface

Lime – Lima

Mango – Manga

Melon – Melão

Mushroom – Cogumelo

Onion – Cebola

Orange – Laranja

Papaya – Papaia / BR: Mamão

Passion fruit – Maracujá

Pea(s) – Ervilha(s)

Peach – Pêssego

Peanut – Amendoim

Pear – Pêra

Pineapple – Ananás / BR: Abacaxi

Raisin(s) – Passa(s)

Salad – Salada

Strawberry / Strawberries – Morango(s)

Spinach – Espinafre

Tomato(es) – Tomate(s)

Watermelon – Melancia

Food and drinks

Bean(s) – Feijão / Feijões

Beef – Carne de vaca / BR: Carne de boi

Beer – Cerveja

Bread – Pão

Butter – Manteiga

Cheese – Queijo

Chicken – Frango

Fish – Peixe

French fries – Batatas fritas

Ham – Fiambre / BR: Presunto

Ice cream – Gelado / BR: Sorvete

Juice – Sumo / BR: Suco

Mashed potatoes – Puré de batata

Meat – Carne

Milk – Leite

Pasta – Massa

Pizza – Pizza

Pork – Carne de porco

Potato – Batata

Rice – Arroz

Salty – Salgado

Soda – Refrigerante

Soup – Sopa

Steak – Bife

Sweet – Doce

Tea – Chá

Water – Água

(Sparkling) water – Água (com gás)

Wine – Vinho

(Red) wine – Vinho (tinto)

(White) wine – Vinho (branco)

General vocabulary and phrases

Bottle – Garrafa

(Wine) bottle – Garrafa de (vinho)

Cook – Cozinheiro

Cup – Chávena / BR: Xícara

(Coffee) cup – Chávena (de café) / BR: Xícara (de café)

(Tea) cup – Chávena (de chá) / BR: Xícara (de chá)

Dessert – Sobremesa

Dinner – Jantar

Dish of the day – Prato do dia / BR: Diária

Entrée – Entradas; Aperitivos

Fork – Garfo

Glass – Copo

Knife – Faca

Lunch – Almoço

Main course – Prato principal

Meal – Refeição

Menu – Ementa / BR: Menu

Plate – Prato

Restaurant - Restaurante

Side dish – Acompanhamento

Spoon – Colher

Table – Mesa

Waiter – Empregado de mesa / BR: Garçon

Wine list – Carta dos vinhos

What's the dish of the day? – Qual é o prato do dia? / BR: Qual é a diária?

Do you have a table for four? – Tem mesa para quatro?

Can you bring the check, please? – Pode trazer a conta, por favor?

8.12.7 At the hospital

Body parts

Ankle(s) – Tornozelo(s)

Appendix – Apêndice

Arm(s) – Braço(s)

Buttocks – Nádegas

Chest – Peito

Elbow(s) – Cotovelo(s)

Eye(s) – Olho(s)

Finger(s) – Dedo(s)

Foot / Feet – Pé(s)

Hand(s) – Mão(s)

Head – Cabeça

Heart – Coração

Hip(s) – Anca(s)

Intestines – Intestinos

Knee(s) – Joelho(s)

Leg(s) – Perna(s)

Liver – Fígado

Lung(s) – Pulmão / Pulmões

Mouth – Boca

Neck – Pescoço

Nose – Nariz

Skin – Pele

Thigh(s) – Coxa(s)

Throat – Garganta

Toe(s) – Dedo(s) do pé

Tongue – Língua

General vocabulary and expressions

Ambulance – Ambulância

Blood type – Tipo sanguíneo

Cold – Constipação; Gripe

Cough – Tosse

Doctor – Doutor

Heart attack – Enfarto; ataque cardíaco

Hospital – Hospital

Infection – Infeção

Nurse – Enfermeiro(a)

Patient – Paciente

Prescription – Receita

Symptom – Sintoma

Stroke – Trombose; AVC; Derrame

Treatment – Tratamento

Waiting room – Sala de espera

Could you call a doctor, please? – Pode chamar um medico, por favor?

I'm not feeling well. – Não me estou a sentir bem. / BR: Não estou me sentindo bem.

I have fever. – Tenho febre. / BR: Estou com febre.

I'm diabetic. – Sou diabético(a).

I'm lactose intolerant. – Sou intolerante à lactose.

The doctor prescribed this medicine. – O doutor receitou este medicamento / remédio.

My ___ hurts. – Sinto uma dor no(a) ___ .

My chest hurts. – Sinto uma dor no peito.

My head hurts. – Sinto uma dor na cabeça.

I'm allergic to peanuts. – Sou alérgico a amendoins.

Conclusion

Now that you've learned the major aspects related to the Portuguese language, all you need to do is practice. When talking to people, it is normal that you feel a little confused at first since you're not used to hear the accent and your brain needs to adapt to it. But don't be scared. If you keep on training, pretty soon you'll get used to it and things will begin to make more sense.

Explore, search, listen, talk, as much as you can. Don't let anything stop you if you really have the willingness to learn. Commit and you'll see the outcome.

To achieve better and faster results you should start by changing your mindset. Try to start thinking in Portuguese as much as you can. In the beginning you will experience some frustration because things won't come to you in a very intuitive manner. But then use this book as a guide and try to overcome that difficulty. If you want to express a thought and you can't find the help you need here, go online and try to figure it out. Don't let any kind of doubt rest in your mind. Over time, you should start to think about things more clearly and your thoughts and speech will begin to flow more naturally.

If you also want to work on your accent the best way to do that is to get used to listen to Portuguese (through interviews, songs, movies, etc.), either the European Portuguese or the Brazilian Portuguese. Since they're considerably different from each other, specially in terms of pronunciation, my advice is that you pick one and try to master it the best way you can. Once you feel comfortable with that accent, and if you want to, go ahead and explore the other one.

Portuguese is a very rich language and you will only benefit if you decide to study both dialects.

Also, if you need an extra drive why don't you encourage some friends and try to immerse them in this journey as well? That will certainly give you one more reason to learn and will motivate you to go forward. The important thing is: never give up.

Think of this learning process as a path that will give you access to another universe, a whole new world of people, culture, stories, and inspirations that can change the way you perceive the world or even introduce you to a new one!

"If you talk to a man in a language he understands, that goes to his head. If you talk to him in his own language, that goes to his heart."

– Nelson Mandela

Preview of Portuguese Short Stories

9 Simple and Captivating Stories for Effective Portuguese Learning for Beginners

Introduction

"He who learns a new language, acquires a new soul." – Czech Proverb

And how immensely valuable would that be?

It opens doors throughout the whole world to different cultures and perspectives; to unknown realities and environments; to unusual customs and beliefs, which will ultimately boil down into one truth – that in spite of all differences we might find, we are, in fact, all very much alike. The gift of being able to communicate, meaning, to understand and to be understood by others, comes with a tremendous responsibility, one that offers two paths:

– One of using words to incite and feed hate and bigotry;

– One of using words to build a bridge between communities.

With that in mind, you are invited to learn the beautiful language that is Portuguese. Being a Romance language, it originates from Latin, just like French, Spanish or Italian. You might find that these languages share common traits, and are very similar in various aspects. That being said, mastering Portuguese might just be the solid foundation from which you can build your knowledge of other Latin–based languages.

It is generally said that there is nothing better when it comes to learning a language than to live in it, to surround yourself with it, to throw yourself into that adventure and just try your best to deliver your message, to find your voice and understand others. That is exactly what *Portuguese Short Stories for Beginners* tries to do. The approach that is adopted is not an intensive reading type of textbook – with customized sentences, constructed to teach bits of the language's rules and structure. It is, instead, an extensive reading type of book that presents the reader with nine short stories that, although not long enough to become boring or dull, have the sufficient length to engage and captivate the reader, whilst displaying fluent and natural Portuguese dialogue. In fact, it has long been regarded as one of the best methods to teach a foreign language.

In addition, this book changed several structured aspects that these kinds of books tend to follow. The reader is confronted with rich and new but not too complex vocabulary, which is translated at the end of the chapter, avoiding the hassle of having to stop the reading rhythm to look up every word in the dictionary. Every paragraph is translated, as well as the summary of the story, thus providing a clearer comprehension of each sentence, while trying to prevent the temptation that the reader might have, if discouraged, of giving up and reading the whole story in English.

After each chapter, there is a question section, which aims to test the reader's overall understanding of the story, containing both open–ended and multiple–choice questions. The solved questions are provided at the end, enabling you to check your own answers and, consequently, develop your skills.

TIPS TO GUIDE YOU THROUGH THE BOOK

Just before you start, here are some tips on how to read the stories more effectively, and a guide on how to solve the questions that are proposed after each chapter, in order to get the most out of the book. There are two different approaches that the learner can adopt whilst reading this book.

The first method is the most regular one:

1. Start by reading the whole story, underlining every word you do not recognize;

2. Then read the translated summary and the vocabulary list. After that, re–read the story. Still, if you do not know the meaning of a particular word that is not in the list, now is the perfect time to look it up in the dictionary. Do not just translate it. A word can have more than one meaning, so it would be useful to see the word used in a sentence;

3. After doing this, read the text as many times as you need to in order to fully comprehend the story and its meaning. Write down any notes or commentaries that you might find to be useful and helpful details, as you go along;

4. When answering the questions, revisit the paragraphs that the question is related to.

The second method is a rather unorthodox one:

1. First, go to the questions section and try to answer them the best you can.

2. Go to the vocabulary list, and try to guess what the words mean. Then check the translation.

3. After that, read the story. With the information you have from the questions that were asked, you already know what you are

looking for, making it easier to figure out the context of the story, the meaning of its words, while managing to increase your focus on the content, and thus becoming more engaged with the story.

With that in mind, but without overthinking it, start this journey with the exciting feeling of knowing that, much more than learning a new language, you are acquiring a new soul!

So, just relax, have fun and good luck!

Boa sorte!

Chapter 1 – Voltar a Casa

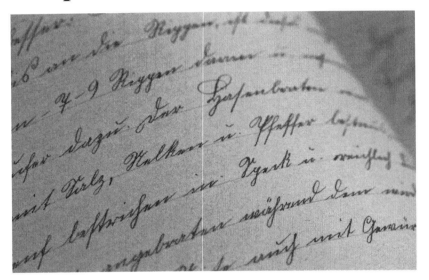

Roberto era o novo aluno na escola secundária de Albufeira, no Algarve. Roberto era um rapaz normal. Tinha 16 anos. Na escola, todos gostavam dele, desde colegas e professores a funcionários e **porteiros**. Era **bem–educado** e **afável**. No entanto, as aulas **aborreciam–no** imenso. Tinha pouco interesse nas **matérias** tratadas, o que fazia com que estivesse **desatento** muitas vezes, entretido a viajar pela sua imaginação. Tinha como principal **passatempo**, depois de acabar os trabalhos de casa, ler. Escolhia um dos livros da biblioteca e era lá que passava a tarde. Para quem o conhecia, tudo nele indicava ser um rapaz como os outros. Com os mesmos problemas e preocupações; com os mesmos interesses e ocupações; não se destacava, nem pela positiva, nem pela negativa. Roberto era, **aparentemente**, um rapaz normal.

Roberto was the new student at Albufeira's high school, in Algarve. Roberto was a normal boy. He was 16 years old. In school, everyone liked him, from colleagues and teachers to workers and doormen. He was polite and nice. However, the classes bored him. He had little interest in the subjects covered, which often made him lose focus in class, being busy traveling on his own mind. He had as his major hobby, after finishing his homework, reading. He would pick a book from the library and spend the afternoon there. For those who knew him, everything about him seemed to be normal, just like the other boys. With the same problems and preoccupations; with the same interests and occupations; he didn't stand out, not in a positive or negative way. Roberto was, apparently, a normal boy.

– Roberto, aqui está o teu teste. Tiveste 73%. Acho que está **aquém** do teu potencial – disse a sua professora, a Senhora Neves.

– Roberto, here's your test. You scored 73%. I think it doesn't match your potential, – said his teacher, Mrs. Neves.

– Obrigada, Senhora Neves. Vou estudar mais para o próximo. – respondeu Roberto.

– Thank you, Mrs. Neves. I'm going to study more for the next one, – answered Roberto.

A professora de Português, a Senhora Neves, tinha sempre visto grande potencial no Roberto, e tratava de o incentivar a fazer melhor. Percebia que ele estava desmotivado pela falta de interesse na escola, e que isso o levava a não se dedicar o suficiente no estudo para ser um excelente aluno. O pouco que estudava chegava era suficiente para passar nos testes, mas sem excelência. Por tudo isto, a professora sentia que o seu talento estava a ser desperdiçado para escrever e criar

histórias . É que o Roberto escrevia sempre as melhores **composições**. Tinha uma capacidade criativa muito superior à dos seus colegas. O seu domínio do Português era muito avançado para alguém da sua idade, tinha um poder de imaginação **invejável**, e uma técnica de descrição de cenários imaginados comparável apenas a **escritores consagrados**. A Senhora Neves adivinhava, e bem, que Roberto devia ler imenso, e que esse devia ser o motivo por detrás de tão **alargado** vocabulário. Supunha igualmente que era dos livros que lia que Roberto retirava o material que o inspirava a criar as suas tão **malucas** e originais histórias. Mas a professora de Roberto não podia estar mais enganada. No mesmo dia em que entregou os testes, decidiu falar com ele no final do dia para tentar ajudá–lo a estudar mais, a perceber como poderia criar aulas mais interessantes, e por último, para perceber como incentivá–lo a tornar–se o grande escritor que ela acreditava que ele podia ser. Depois da sua última aula, foi para a biblioteca, porque tinha a certeza que, como todos os outros dias, era lá que Roberto ia estar. E, efectivamente, lá estava Roberto, na sua mesa habitual, ao pé da janela.

The Portuguese teacher, Mrs. Neves, had always seen a great potential in Roberto, and she motivated him to do better. She understood that he wasn't motivated because he wasn't interested in school, which led him to not put enough effort into being an excellent student. What he did was enough to pass the tests, but he didn't excel in them. Because of all of this, Mrs. Neves felt that he was wasting his talent to write and create stories. Roberto was always the one who wrote the best essays. His creative skills were far superior than those of his colleagues. His mastery of Portuguese was really advanced for someone his age, his imaginative power was enviable, and his technique to describe made up worlds was only comparable to acclaimed writers. Mrs. Neves rightly guessed that Roberto must read a lot, and that was the cause of such rich vocabulary. She also assumed that it was from the books that he read that Roberto got his inspiration to create such crazy and original stories. But Roberto's teacher couldn't be more mistaken. The same day she gave the tests back to her class, she decided she was going to talk to him at the end of the day, to motivate him to study more, to understand how she could make the classes more interesting, and, at last, to understand how she could help him become the great writer that she believed he could be. After her last class, she went to the library, because she knew that, like every other day, Roberto was going to be there. And Roberto was indeed there, sitting at his usual table, near the window.

– Olá Roberto, importas–te que me sente aqui contigo? – perguntou a Senhora Neves.

– Hi Roberto, do you mind me sitting here with you? – asked Mrs. Neves.

– Não, Senhora Neves, esteja à vontade. – respondeu Roberto, educado como sempre.

– No, Mrs. Neves, please do, – answered Roberto, polite as always.

– Sentas–te sempre nesta mesa, à janela. É para veres as **miúdas giras** que passam? – brincou a Senhora Neves.

– You always sit at this table, by the window. It's to look at cute girls passing by? – joked Mrs. Neves.

O Roberto sorriu. Ele gostava da Senhora Neves. Era acessível, mas fazia–se sempre respeitar. Era assertiva, sem ser demasiado rígida. Era compreensiva e tolerante, mantendo sempre a sua autoridade.

Roberto smiled. He liked Mrs. Neves. She was approachable, but everyone respected her. She was assertive, without being too stiff. She was understanding and tolerant, always maintaining her authority.

– Não... Quer dizer, também passam miúdas giras, e eu olho, claro, mas eu gosto de estar aqui para ver a **paisagem**... Para ver como o vento bate nas folhas das árvores; como a chuva deixa a **relva molhada** e triste; como o sol faz brilhar as flores... E os sorrisos dessas miúdas giras! – respondeu Roberto.

– No… I mean, there are cute girls passing by, and I look at them, of course, but what I like about being here is looking at the view… to watch how the wind blows the leaves; how the rain leaves the grass wet and sad; how the sun makes the flowers shine… and the smiles of those cute girls! – answered Roberto.

– Ah, estou a ver! O poder de observação… Foi assim que aprendeste a descrever tão bem cenários e objectos! É daqui que imaginas todas as histórias? Aquela do rapazinho que é um extraterrestre – onde foste buscar a inspiração para esse **conto**? – perguntou, curiosa, a Senhora Neves.

– Oh, I see! The power of observation… That's how you learned to describe the scenarios and objects! It's from here that you imagine all the stories? The one of the boy who's an alien – where did you get the inspiration for that tale? – asked, Mrs. Neves full of curiosity.

Roberto não sabia se devia dizer a verdade. Sentia, verdadeiramente, que podia confiar na professora, mas isto era um segredo demasiado forte. Já há tanto tempo que o guardava, que isso o consumia. Tinha uma enorme vontade de **desabafar** e falar disso, de pedir ajuda. **Não obstante**, sentia o peso do segredo e a responsabilidade que tinha de o contar. Tomou uma decisão.

Roberto didn't know if he should tell the truth. He truly felt that he could trust Mrs. Neves, but this was a strong secret to tell. He had kept it for so long that it was devouring him. He felt the need to vent and talk about it, to ask for help. However, he also felt the weight of the secret he was carrying and the responsibility of telling it. He made a decision.

– Bem, Prof., eu leio muito, e vou juntando pedaços de diferentes livros. E depois, com as minhas fantasias, crio uma história. – mentiu Roberto.

– Well, Mrs. Neves, I read a lot, and I put together pieces of different books. And then, with my fantasies, I create a story, - lied Roberto.

– Muito bem, muito bem. Eu gostei muito desse conto em particular. Mas olha, eu vim aqui sentar–me contigo para falar sobre uma coisa... Noto que andas desmotivado, sem muito interesse nas aulas. Tens um potencial muito grande, e vejo que gostas realmente de escrever. Iria fazer-me muito triste, e tu também, penso eu, se não cumprisses o sonho, se é que tens esse sonho, de seres escritor. Acredito **verdadeiramente** que és **capaz**, e que podes ter muito sucesso. Tenho razão quando digo que tens esse sonho, não tenho? – inquiriu a Senhora Neves.

– Very well, very well. I liked this tale particularly. But I came here and sat with you to talk to you about something... I can tell you haven't been motivated, no interest at all in class. You have a great potential, and I can tell you really like to write. It would make me very sad, and you, too, I think, if you didn't achieve your dream, that is if you have this dream of being a writer. I truly believe that you can do it, and that you can be very successful. I'm right when I say that you do have this dream, am I not? – asked Mrs. Neves.

– Sim, tem toda a razão... Eu sempre quis ser escritor, desde que me lembro, desde que comecei a ler. Mas eu tenho interesse nas aulas! É verdade que me tenho sentido um pouco triste... Porque não é assim tão fácil ... Não para mim, pelo menos. – respondeu Roberto.

– Yeah, you're totally right... I had always wanted to be a writer, ever since I can remember, ever since I started to read. But I do have interest in the classes! It's true that I have been feeling a bit sad... Because it's not that easy... Not for me, at least, – answered Roberto.

– Com certeza que não é fácil Roberto, não é fácil para ninguém. Para ti será a mesma coisa. Mas tu tens um talento extraordinário e gostas do que fazes. Raras vezes isso se conjuga. Acho que seria uma oportunidade que estarias a **desperdiçar** se pelo menos não tentasses. – disse a Senhora Neves.

– Of course it's not easy Roberto, it's not easy for anyone. For you it is the same thing. But you do have an extraordinary talent and you like what you do. It's very unusual for that to happen. I think that this is an opportunity you would be wasting, if you didn't at least try, – said Mrs. Neves.

– Sim, mas quando digo que não é fácil, refiro-me a outra coisa... – explicou o Roberto.

– Yeah, but when I say that it's not easy, I meant something else… – explained Roberto.

– Do que estás a falar, então? – a Senhora Neves não estava a acompanhar o **raciocínio** de Roberto, e agora, mais que nunca, sentia que algo se passava.

– So, what are you talking about then? – Mrs. Neves wasn't following Roberto's train of thought, and now, more than ever, she felt that something was going on.

Roberto já não aguentava mais. A professora mostrava interesse nele, na vida dele, no que ele pensava e sentia. Era a pessoa ideal para desabafar e finalmente confessar toda a verdade.

Roberto couldn't take it anymore. Mrs. Neves showed interest in him, in his life, in what he thought and felt. She was the ideal person to vent out and finally confess all the truth.

– A história que escrevi sobre o menino de Plutão que tinha vindo para a Terra é verdade. É tudo **verdade**, nada imaginado. Esse menino sou eu – eu sou o Ragnikako Lopve. Por isso descrevo tão bem algo que julga inventado, por isso crio **enredos** e objectos tão malucos – porque tudo é real e existe, no meu planeta.

– The story that I wrote about the boy from Pluto who came to Earth is true. It was all true, nothing was made up. That boy is me – I'm Ragnikako Lopve. That's why I describe so well something you think is made up, that's why I create such crazy stories and objects – because everything is real and exists, in my planet.

O sentimento de **alívio** tomou conta dele. Roberto sentia que tinham retirado um **fardo** gigantesco dos seus ombros. A Senhora Neves, embora ainda um pouco chocada pela revelação, viu a cara de Roberto e a maneira como ele suspirou quando partilhou o seu grande segredo. Começou a importar-se ainda mais, porque confiou nela ao ponto de confessar informação tão importante e pessoal. O Roberto começou, pois, a contar toda a sua história. Que o seu avô, um famoso astronauta de Plutão, tinha visitado a Terra muitos anos antes, e tinha trazido como **oferenda** para o seu líder 10 livros em Português, exibidos no museu Galáctico de Plutão. Contou-lhe que no seu planeta a linguagem era **gestual**, não havia palavras escritas ou faladas. Que foi o seu avô, que aprendeu a língua portuguesa no tempo que passou em Portugal, que o ensinou a ler e a escrever, e que daí nasceu a sua vontade de ser escritor. Com esse sonho no seu coração, despediu–se da sua família e deixou o seu planeta, para fazer a longa viagem até ao planeta Terra, e cumprir o seu destino.

A feeling of relief took over him. Roberto felt that someone had taken a burden off his shoulders. Mrs. Neves, although still a little shocked by the revelation, saw Roberto's face and the way he breathed when he shared his big secret. She started caring even more, because he trusted her enough to share such an important and personal piece of information. Roberto then started telling all of his story. That his grandfather, a famous astronaut from Pluto, had visit the Earth many years earlier, and that he had brought back, as an offering for his leader, 10 books in Portuguese, which were displayed in the Pluto Galactic museum. He told her that in his planet, they had sign language, there wasn't written or spoken words. That his grandfather, who learnt the Portuguese language in his time in Portugal, was the one who taught him how to read and write, and from that originated his desire to become a writer. With that dream in his heart, he kissed his family goodbye and left his planet, to make the long journey to Earth and fulfill his destiny.

A Senhora Neves já sabia a maior parte das coisas, porque tinha lido a composição que Roberto escreveu. Ia–lhe fazendo perguntas quando tinha dúvidas, e estava ainda completamente supreendida pela realidade da situação. No entanto, havia um questão que a **atormentava** mais que todas as outras.

Mrs. Neves knew about most of the things, since she had read the essay that Roberto wrote. She asked him some questions, now and again, and she was still completely surprised about the reality of the situation. However, there was a question that was tormenting her, more than any other.

– Mas Roberto, porque tens andado tão triste ultimamente? Estás aqui a lutar pelo teu sonho, e tens a capacidade para o atingir! – interrogou-se a professora.

– But Roberto, why have you been so sad lately? You're here pursuing your dream, and you have the skills to achieve it! – wondered Mrs. Neves.

– Porque cada dia tenho mais tenho saudades de casa e da minha família. Quando lá estava, só pensava em fugir dali e viajar... A única coisa que eu queria na vida era ser escritor. Mas agora, só penso que abdicaria disso para poder ver e viver com a minha família outra vez. – confessou Roberto. – E no fundo, sei que quando lá estivesse, depois de um certo tempo, quereria voltar e ser escritor... E assim seria a minha vida para sempre... Eu sei que não se pode ter tudo, mas...

– Because everyday I miss my home and my family more and more. When I was there, I only thought about running away and travel... The only thing I wanted to do in life was to be a writer. But now, I would give all of that up to see and be with my family again, – confessed Roberto. – And deep down, I know if I were there, after some time, I would want to come back and be a writer... And that is how my life would be for ever... I know we can't have it all, but...

Os olhos da Senhora Neves brilharam, como quando alguém tem uma brilhante ideia. Estava a considerar cada passo da decisão que acabava de tomar. Tinha a certeza que ia ser um excelente **conselho**.

Mrs. Neves's eyes shone, just like when someone has a brilliant idea. She was considering every step of the decision she had just made. She was sure it was going to be good advice.

– No que está a pensar, Senhora Neves? – perguntou, **intrigado** mas entusiasmado, o Roberto. É que a excitação da Senhora Neves **transbordava**, mesmo antes de falar.

– What are you thinking about, Mrs. Neves? – asked Roberto, intrigued but excited. Mrs. Neves's was overflowing with excitement, even before she talked.

– O que achas de voltar a casa e ser também escritor? – perguntou a
Senhora Neves.

– What do you think about going back home, and being a writer as
well? – asked Mrs. Neves.

– Acho que seria perfeito, mas infelizmente, impossível... Lá não
tenho livros para ler, nem folhas para escrever. Além disso, ninguém
sabe Português, ninguém saberia ler o que eu escrevesse. – respondeu
desanimado Roberto.

– I think that would be perfect, but unfortunately, impossible. I don't
have books to read there, or even paper to write on. Besides, nobody
knows Portuguese, nobody would know how to read what I wrote. –
answered Roberto, discouraged.

– É aí que eu te posso ajudar. Eu tenho uma biblioteca pessoal em
casa. É enorme e tem muito valor – e pode ser tua, se quiseres. O meu
plano era: levavas todos esses livros contigo, e muitas folhas em
branco para escrever. Abrias uma escola e ensinavas Português em
Plutão. E assim, podias ter livros para ler, folhas para escrever, e uma
comunidade que entendesse Português para ler os teus livros. Quem
sabe quantos alunos poderias inspirar e ajudar a ser escritores
também!...

– I can help you with that. I have a personal library at home. It's enormous and is of great value – and it could be yours, if you want it. My plan was: you would take all of those books with you, and a lot of white paper to write. You would open a school there and teach Portuguese in Pluto. With that, you could have books to read, papers to write, and a community who understood Portuguese that could read your books. Who knows how many students you could also inspire and help to become writers!...

– Como a professora me inspirou e ajudou a mim!... – disse o **emocionado** Roberto. – Nunca vou esquecer o que fez por mim! *Nunca*!

– The way you inspired and helped me!... – said Roberto, moved. – I'll never forget what you did for me! *Never!*

– Está decidido! Obrigado... És um miúdo incrível! E também nunca te vou esquecer. – respondeu, **comovida**, a Senhora Neves, tocada pelo que ele disse. – Desculpa, mas tenho mais uma pergunta: como é que vais para casa?

– It's set! Thank you… You're an amazing kid! And I too will never forget you. – answered Mrs. Neves, touched by what he said. – I'm sorry, but I have one more question: how are you going to get home?

– Ah, professora, esse é o único segredo que não posso mesmo revelar! – disse o Roberto, com um sorriso misterioso.

– Oh, Mrs. Neves, that's the only secret I can't really reveal! – said Roberto, with a mysterious grin.

Assim voltou Roberto para Plutão. Reencontrou–se com a sua família, que o recebeu de braços abertos. Todos os livros que trouxe da Terra ficaram em exposição no museu Galáctico e as gentes de Plutão tinham muito interesse em ver aquela biblioteca. Abriu uma escola, onde tinha alunos novos e velhos. Todos, sem excepção, se **apaixonaram** pelo Português. Muitos começaram a escrever as suas próprias histórias. Roberto cumpriu também o seu sonho de ser escritor, e era **idolatrado** pela população do seu planeta. Fez exactamente o que a professora planeou e **previu**, e **disfrutava** de uma vida muito, muito feliz.

And so Roberto returned to Pluto. He reunited with his family, who received him with open arms. Every book that he brought from Earth was displayed in the Galactic museum, and the people from Pluto were very interested in seeing that library. He opened a school, where there were young and old students. Everyone, without exception, fell in love with Portuguese. Many started to write their own stories. Roberto fulfilled his dream of becoming a writer and was idolized by his people. He did exactly what his teacher planned out and predicted, and he was enjoying a really, really happy life.

Anos mais tarde, já estava a Senhora Neves **reformada**, quando recebeu uma **encomenda** no correio. Era um livro, com uma capa estranha. Abriu–o, e na primeira página dizia:

Years later, a retired Mrs. Neves received a package in the mail. It was a book, with a weird cover. She opened it, and in the first page it said:

"Para a melhor professora do mundo – do Roberto, um rapaz normal."

"For the best teacher in the world – from Roberto, a normal boy."

Afinal, Ragnikako Lopve não se tinha esquecido dela.

After all, Ragnikako Lopve really did not forget about her.

Sumário

Roberto era como um rapaz normal. Era bem–educado e simpático e todos gostavam dele. O seu sonho era ser escritor, e tinha um grande talento e potencial. As suas capacidades criativas eram especiais, e o seu domínio da língua invejável. No entanto, guardava um segredo que ninguém conhecia, e que o estava a fazer sentir miserável. O seu dilema era grande demais para não ser partilhado, e precisava desesperadamente do apoio e ajuda de alguém. Por coincidência, tinha uma professora fantástica, que via nele um escritor promissor e acreditava no seu futuro brilhante. Preocupava–se com ele, o que fez com que este se sentisse à vontade para desabafar com a sua professora e contar tudo o que preocupava. Ela ofereceu–se imediatamente para ajudar e teve um brilhante ideia, o que resultou numa grande felicidade para os dois, fazendo com que Roberto cumprisse o seu eterno sonho, sem estar longe daqueles que mais amava. Ficou eternamente grato à professora pela sua ajuda.

Summary

Roberto was like a normal boy. He was polite and nice and everyone liked him. His dream was to be a writer, and he had great talent and potential. His creative skills were special, and his mastery of the language was enviable. However, he kept a secret that nobody was aware of, and that was making him feel miserable. His dilemma was too big not to be shared, and he desperately needed somebody's support and help. By coincidence, he had a fantastic teacher, who saw in him a promising writer and that believed in his bright future. She worried about him, and that made him feel comfortable enough to vent with his teacher and tell her everything that was going on. She offered her help immediately and had a brilliant idea that resulted in great happiness for both, which enabled Roberto to fulfil his dream, while being near those whom he loved. He was eternally grateful to his teacher for her help.

Vocabulary List

Porteiros – doormen, gatekeepers

Bem–educado – polite

Afável – affable

Aborreciam–no – bored him

Matérias – subjects

Desatento – inattentive, absent–minded

Passatempo – pastime, hobby

Aparentemente – apparently

Aquém – below, fall short

Histórias – stories

Desperdiçado – wasted

Composições – essays

Invejável – enviable

Escritores – writers

Consagrados – established, acclaimed

Alargado – widened (but in this case it means large, broad)

Malucas – crazy, insane, mad

Miúdas giras – cute girls

Paisagem – view, landscape

Relva – grass

Molhada – wet

Conto – short story

Desabafar – vent

Não obstante – however

Verdadeiramente – truly

Capaz – able, capable

Cabisbaixo – sad, crestfallen

Desperdiçar – wasting

Raciocínio – reasoning, train of thought

Verdade – truth

Enredos – plots

Alívio – relief

Fardo – burden

Tamanho – such (in this context)

Acréscimo – increase

Oferenda – offering, gift

Gestual – sign (language)

Atormentava – tormented

Conselho – advice

Intrigado – intrigued

Transbordava – overflowing, bursting, overfilling

Desanimado – discouraged

Emocionado – moved or touched

Comovida – also moved or touched

Apaixonaram – fell in love

Idolatrado – idolized, worshipped

Previu – predicted

Desfrutava – enjoyed

Reformada – retired

Encomenda – package

Continue reading

PORTUGUESE
SHORT STORIES

9 SIMPLE AND CAPTIVATING STORIES FOR
EFFECTIVE PORTUGUESE
LEARNING FOR BEGINNERS

LANGUAGE LEARNING UNIVERSITY

Check out this book!

Printed in Great Britain
by Amazon

46102541R00090